STILL TRUE TO TYPE

An Introduction to Type and Answers to the Most Frequently Asked Questions About Completing and Interpreting the Myers-Briggs Type Indicator®

By William C. Jeffries

Author of *Hannibal, Hummers, and Hot Air Balloons: High Performance Strategies for Tough Times, Taming the Scorpion: Preparing Business for the Third Millennium,* and *True to Type*

™

Buttermilk Ridge Publishing

Published by:
Buttermilk Ridge Publishing
136 S. 9th Street, Ste 18
Noblesville, IN 46060
www.buttermilkridgepublishing.com

Distributed by:
Executive Strategies International, Inc.
9620 Irishman's Run Lane
Zionsville, Indiana 46077
www.execustrat.com

Library of Congress Control Number 2002111915
Jeffries, William C.
    Still True to Type / William C. Jeffries
        p.   cm.
    ISBN 0-9723961-1-X

Back cover photo by Jennifer Marshall, MG Photography.

Printed in the USA

Dedication

Once more, for my children: Tiffany, Ainsley, Joshua, Austin, and Paul. Each very different, each a different challenge, and each a part of my heart.

Every day you remind me anew about the beauty, power, and richness of the incredible diversity in our lives. Thank you!

TABLE OF CONTENTS

INDEX TO QUESTIONS

12. Why do several questions seem to ask the same thing? p. 67.

13. Are intuitives more creative than sensors? p. 68.

14. What do very high scores or very low scores indicate about a person? Which is better? p. 72.

15. What does "Balance" mean in Type theory? p. 75.

16. Can the MBTI® be used for psychologically disturbed people? p. 76.

17. Do "TJ's" make the best senior managers? p. 78.

18. How effective can the MBTI® be in reflecting the Types of individuals from different cultures and nationalities? p. 81.

19. What are word pairs, and why do some people report this data to the client? p. 87.

20. My preference for Introversion has gotten stronger the older I have become. Is that unusual? p. 89.

21. Are there any discernible racial differences or patterns reflected in our types? p. 90.

22. Some consultants use letter combinations of "ST," "SF," "NF," & "NT." Others use "SJ" and "SP" in lieu of "ST" & "SF." What is the difference? p. 91.

23. What is meant by "falsification of type"? p. 93.

37. Why do some of us who are Extraverts have such a hard time introducing ourselves to others or sharing personal insights during meetings? Aren't we supposed to be gregarious and friendly? p. 125.

38. I have heard some people talk about working out of their "Shadow" function. What does that mean? p. 128.

39. How often should I retake the MBTI®? p. 129.

40. Can't I make the MBTI® come out any Type I want? p. 130.

41. Are any of my four letters more or less influential than the others? p. 131.

42. Can I use Type to hire the right person for a job? p. 133.

43. Should I use my Type to choose a career? p. 134.

44. Does being an "F" mean that I am more emotional than my "T" associates? p. 135.

45. Sixteen types are a lot to remember. Do you have any tips for remembering what all these letters mean? p. 136.

46. How does the MBTI® compare with the DISC? p. 137.

47. I have read criticism from time to time that suggests the MBTI® is little more than a quaint parlor game because all it indicates is positive "traits" about a person. What do you say? p. 138.

managing related to psychological type? p. 163.

60. How can we use Type most effectively in managerial coaching? p. 164.

61. Have the questions on the indicator always been the same and, if I take the indicator repeated times, are there alternate versions of the form? p. 165.

62. Who are some famous people I can reference as examples of Type? p. 175.

63. Is the Enneagram related to Type? p. 177.

64. What is an archetype, and how does it differ from a Type? p. 178.

65. Now that we have typed the team or the organization, what is the next step? p. 179.

66. Now that I know my type, how can I type my family? p. 182

QUESTIONS GROUPED BY CATEGORIES

Numbers indicate questions beginning on page 45.
The Concept of Preferences: 1, 11, 23, 26, 41, 44, & 50.

Psychometrics and Scientific Credibility: 4, 9, 10, 12, 19, & 27.

The History of the Indicator: 3, 51, 52, & 61.

Correlation between the Indicator and Other Systems: 8, 46, & 63.

Completing the Indicator: 39 & 40.

Developmental Issues: 2, 6, 7, 20, 25, & 29.

Consulting With the Indicator: 45, 47, 48, 49, 57, 60, & 62.

Teaming Uses of the Indicator: 5, 14, 32, 33, 55, & 65.

Organizational Applications of the Indicator: 13, 17, 22, 36, 43, 48, 49, 53, 54, & 59.

Health Issues: 16 & 34.

Education and Training: 56 & 58.

Population Norms and Cross Cultural Implications: 18, 21, 28, & 30.

Ethical Issues: 31, 35, & 42.

Advanced Jungian Implications: 15, 24, 37, 38, & 64.

Consulting With The Indicator: 45, 47, 48, 49, 57, 60, & 65.

ACKNOWLEDGEMENTS

Anyone writing about psychological type today has a host of predecessors who have contributed to our general knowledge. Our collective special debt is to Katharine C. Briggs and Isabel Briggs Myers who brought the theory of type to life and to Dr. Mary H. McCaulley who has done so much in her lifetime to perpetuate the authors' ideas and to work to help establish the intellectual and professional credibility of the theory through her research and collaboration.

My colleagues all deserve tremendous credit for enduring for years my pushy INTJ passion for competence. Our ESI learning community has assembled a remarkable cadre of business associates in several countries who challenge one another on a daily basis to be the best we can be. Each of them has contributed significantly to my understanding about type differences. Let me just mention them in the order in which they joined our learning team: Jeff Trenton, Leah Dempsey, Judith Noel, Tom Hoffman, Jerry Rankin, Walt Smith, Dr. Marcy Lawton, Rebecca McCord, Joy Roy, Yolanda Vega, Dr. Richard Kimball, Pat Ross, Dr. Richard Bents, Dr. Eugene Dorris, Dr. Reiner Blank, Dr. Ira Rosenberg, Dr. Freeman Barnes, and Hilse Barbosa.

I owe a special debt of gratitude to the millions of people with whom I have worked since first writing *True To Type* in 1990. A partial list of corporations, universities, senior military colleges, government agencies, and consulting firms from 39 countries that have shared data with me over the years is located at Appendix II. You have challenged, stretched, and taught me what it really means to be *True To Type*. I hope I have been faithful to your expectations. My family and yours, as well as all of our employees, have provided me an endless repertoire of stories, examples, and anecdotes that bring type alive every day.

PREFACE

Ten years ago when I wrote *True To Type*, I had been using the Myers-Briggs Type Indicator® (MBTI®) for eight years. About 30% of my clients were corporations in the private sector, but the majority of my clients were members of the five U. S. military services, all federal government agencies, senior military officers from France, Australia, Germany, Belgium, Italy, Saudi Arabia, Turkey, England, Spain, several Latin American countries, and numerous other senior executive associations. As I branched out into the private sector, I had a small network of associates who worked with me in my sole proprietorship business, and I was, quite frankly, amazed at the power of this simple form to capture so well a person's personality preferences. As an engineer who had been systematically trained to scoff at the intangibles of the world, I found the MBTI® a unique bridge between scientific logic and human nuance. And, so, my solitary journey across that bridge began.

Now, a decade later, as the President and CEO of an international consulting and training corporation, I remain as fascinated as I was in the 1980's with the subtle power of the MBTI®, and even more amazed at its versatility and capability to help individuals and organizations learn about themselves. I have traveled that bridge with many of you over the last ten years, and the journey has taken us to 29 countries where we routinely work. I am particularly proud of the networks of associates we have worked with, not only here in North America, but also in Europe, Asia, Africa, and Latin America. In 1990, I never could have imagined that in the third millennium I would leave my current office in the cobblestone village of Zionsville

in rural Indiana for every business trip carrying in my
briefcase copies of the MBTI® in German, Spanish,
Chinese, French, Italian, Portuguese, and, oh by the way,
English.

My publisher has been trying to get me to update *True To
Type* for at least five years. Despite my best intentions,
that hasn't happened. I have been too busy writing other
books related to business high performance and team
building and working with clients to take the time necessary to write. I am not a researcher by inclination. I would
much rather impact lives and relationships and change
organizations than make presentations at conferences and
write articles for magazines. I would also, quite frankly,
rather grow my business than provide information to others so they can grow theirs. Does this sound like any
other INTJ's you might know?

Just as ESI, Inc. employs proprietary business models for
Creating Organizational Mastery, Organizational Change,
and Creating Cultures of High Performance, so our type
data bank is private and is available for the sole business
use of our clients, and much of it will remain proprietary
as long as I remain CEO. What I am willing to share
about those business models is in my 1999 book *Taming
The Scorpion: Preparing American Business for the Third
Millennium*, and my 2001 book, *Hannibal, Hummers, and
Hot Air Balloons: High Performance Strategies for Tough
Times*. Both of these books are available at any on-line
service, good bricks-and-mortar book stores, or from ESI,
Inc. at our corporate website, www.execustrat.com.

At the same time, knowledge of type should be able to
enrich the lives of others—my ENFP, ESFJ, INFP, and
ENFJ colleagues remind me of this sentiment on a daily
basis. They have helped to fuel this impulse to write a little more about type. How to do that has been my dilem-

ma. I will share some of our extensive data on businesses in this book. It will probably not be as much as some of you, including some of my consultants, would like. I will also expand our knowledge about the Jungian implications of our preferences.

True To Type has continued to be very successful, and those of you purchasing it have continued to be very complimentary about not only the contents but also the style—questions and answers that break the topic down into "digestible titrations," as one chemical engineer phrased it. I just finished reading the book again myself for the first time in several years and am pleased to say that aside from the three grammatical errors and two solecisms I came across, there is not one thing I would change about what I said then. I may have been a little naïve from time to time, but I was accurate—for an INTJ that is the chief virtue.

What has changed dramatically is our data bank (which we believe is the largest type data bank in the world, bar none), the applications to which we put the MBTI®, our understanding of cross-cultural implications of personality types around the world, and the ability of "type" as a mental model to grow more effective leaders and to transform businesses. That is what this book is all about. I hope you find it a valuable addition to your library.

Every chapter has been updated and modified to some degree from the first edition. I have also added new chapters on the following uses of type:
- Type and Executive Coaching
- Understanding the many versions available of the MBTI®
- Building the Virtual Team
- Jungian Implications of our Preferences

17

- Type and Leadership Style
- Type and Organizational Profitability and Safety
- Type and Outdoor Adventures
- Learning Disabilities and Type
- Diversity and Type
- Organizational Culture and Type
- The Prediction Ratio
- The Preference Clarity Indicator
- The correlation between the MBTI® and the DISC
- Type and the Enneagram
- Types of Famous People
- The relationship between Types and Archetypes?
- Population Norms
- Types most often found at the Senior Executive Level
- Typing my family and friends
- So you have Typed your Organization or Team— what are the Next Steps?

As in my other books, I encourage you to let me know what you think. Write, call, or better yet, email me with comments, questions, observations, and I will get back to you. I invite you to visit our website at www.execustrat.com, to learn further about our many uses of type. The best e-mail to use to reach me personally is bill.jeffries@execustrat.com. I actually answer all my e-mails myself. In the coming years, I hope to meet you virtually, if not in the flesh. If you are more comfortable with traditional technology, you can still contact me at our present address at 9620 Irishman's Run Lane, Zionsville, Indiana 46077 USA, or call on the POTS at (800) 977-1688.

FOREWORD

In the first edition of *True to Type*, I responded to several questions I had received in my seminars around the world and promised to answer them succinctly and correctly, not necessarily completely. Some of the questions, quite obviously, had been the subject of entire books by other authors. I tried not to repeat what others had already said. I also attempted to eschew the cant of psychometricians in favor of more colloquial speech. I will continue that approach in this revision. The risk I run is that I will not sound scholarly in my answers. If you are accustomed to the arcane jargon of presenters at APT conferences, you will be disappointed with me. For that violation of expectations and decorum, I ask your forgiveness in advance.

What I hope to do is to be totally honest and frank in my responses. That approach doesn't always make some people happy. Some of my answers are based on research, some on experience, and some on conjecture. I will do my best to be clear, in each case, which it is. If I can cite any other authority to help clarify my answers, I will. What I am is a very busy, active consultant who uses type almost every day in Fortune 500 Companies in assignments ranging in variety from Conflict Management, Team Building, and Diversity Education and Training, to Adventure Learning, Executive Coaching, and structuring programs in Culture Change, Business High Performance, and Executive Development.

My interest is not in sitting in a university somewhere dreaming up new demographic questions to put on the reverse side of the MBTI® or pondering new versions of the questionnaire so that anyone who took Form F or G in the past might want to retake the new version for an asymptotically increased fee. My passion is changing organizations and lives, not generating revenue for the publisher of the instrument.

The first edition of *True To Type* targeted those who were familiar with type and wished to grow further. I directed many of my responses to those consulting with type. My focus this time will target those who have completed the MBTI® and had an introduction to type and wish to grow further. ***This, then, should be the first book you read after that introduction to ground you further in the basics of type theory.*** There is also an advanced section to take anyone familiar with type to some important Jungian implications of our preferences.

If you are relatively new to type, I suggest you begin with the section called "An Introduction to Type: What it is and is not." This section will ground you in the basics of the MBTI® or provide you a practical review of what the eight choices actually mean.

AN INTRODUCTION TO TYPE: WHAT IT IS & IS NOT

GENERAL BACKGROUND

If you are relatively new to psychological type and have not had a chance to be involved in a formal feedback session on the Myers-Briggs Type Indicator (MBTI)®, this is the place to start.

The MBTI® is a carefully validated, highly reliable personality inventory that allows individuals to declare the degree to which they express preferences for eight aspects of human personality. It is not, as many consultants and popularizers of the indicator refer to it, a psychological "test." The distinction is important, even though the word "test" is used popularly to describe several such instruments, because the word "test" suggests that the choices on the indicator are somehow related to the categories of right or wrong. It amazes me that some otherwise competent consultants persist in the easy cant of "test" to describe the indicator. The term is confusing and I believe detrimental to the ethical use of the form. Even the copyright holder, Consulting Psychologists Press, has used the words "psychological test" to describe the instrument. Shame on you!

Perhaps no feature of the indicator is as important as this one. Once consultants or trainers begin to psychoanalyze their clients, use the indicator to discuss abilities, predict performance, or in any other way box in, categorize, advantage or disadvantage anyone, they have overstepped their charter. No types are right or wrong, and no types are appropriate or inappropriate for any job. Too often, even when this opinion is not overtly stated, this is the impression that lingers.

Often, what the MBTI® does not measure is more important to convey than what it does measure. I have met many people over the years who were initially reluctant to complete the indicator because in the past they have felt labeled by some other "test": the MMPI, FIRO-B, DISC (Personal profile System), LIFO, etc. As a starting point, I always declare the positive, nonrestrictive nature of the indicator.

Quite simply, the MBTI® reports nothing about intelligence, maturity, development, stress, or possible psychological disturbances. Indeed, as a psychometric instrument based on Carl Jung's theory of personality, it has a "wellness" orientation, not a sickness or pathological orientation. For that reason, it has become the most widely selling psychological inventory on the market today, designed for use with non-psychiatric audiences. Today, according to the publisher, about 3.5 million people take the indicator each year for the first time.

THE EIGHT PREFERENCES
As best we currently can understand people—a murky science at best—we believe that if we strip aside the spiritual aspect of what it means to be human, put that on hold temporarily, then what remains can be described in a fairly scientific way by looking at four things we as humans do: how we see reality, how we judge that view of reality, where we go to get our energy, and how others see our orientation to the world. In each of these four areas of life, there are two dichotomous choices:

Extraversion or Introversion

Sensing or iNtuition

Thinking or Feeling
Judging or Perceiving

According to the theory, all eight preferences are equally valuable. When you complete the instrument, you pick one preference off of each line. The combination of the four choices becomes what we call your Psychological Type.

We report your preference to you on a report form in terms of four letters and a numerical score associated with each preference. The number does not indicate how well or poorly you do anything. It simply indicates the clarity of your preference: Slight, Clear, Moderate, or Very Clear. If you complete the indicator with Executive Strategies International, we also return to you a multiple-page profile of your type to help you validate your choices. See my book *Profiles of the 16 Personality Types*.

Let's walk through the four sets of preferences. Human beings are story-telling creatures. The great bards of the past sang the feats of heroes from Beowulf to Ulysses. Jesus told parables to help people understand the kingdom he was proclaiming, Shakespeare enriched our culture with the stories of tragic and comic figures, and Aesop gave us fables to enrich our moral framework. Business leaders today also have to be able to tell effective stories—call them visions and missions and values—to create high performance. Since we tell stories in our seminars to help participants understand the broad richness of type, here are some you might find helpful.

SENSING OR INTUITION

Because the first question we ask is how we see reality, we always start our presentations describing the "S-N" differences. Sensors see reality in terms of the immediate, the real, the practical facts of life. They prefer to deal with data, facts, and specifics. They bring their perception of reality in through the five senses: what they can see, feel, taste, hear, and smell. Intuitives see the same thing, but instead they register their view of reality in terms of theories, concepts, ideas, possibilities, and relationships among the data.

SOME KEY WORDS:

Sensing	Intuitive
Data & Facts	Ideas
Information	Implication
Specific	Concept
Practical	Possibility
Literal	Symbolic
Concrete	Abstract
Conserve	Change
Literal	Figurative
Directions	Hunches
Utility	Novelty

When "S's" and "N's" wander through the same office, they both see what is, but what they see can be remarkably different. The sensor may see six desks (four of which are occupied at 10:45 am), eleven Hewlett Packard, Omnibook 4150 computers, four Color LaserJet 4500 printers, thirteen AT&T telephones, assorted software lying about, four clerks (2 male, 2 female), stacks of Hammermill white bond paper, three filing cabinets, one water cooler in need of a replacement bottle, nine windows that will not open, two calendars, and a coffee pot brewing some Starbucks Kenya Gold. The intuitive walking through the same office may report seeing an understaffed, crowded office. Which is the correct view of the office? Both, of course, may be equally accurate. Neither is right and neither is wrong, but a more complete description of the office embraces both. The sensor records specifics; the intuitive records meanings. We need both.

Sensors are the literalists of the world; intuitives are more the symbolists and the ones more likely to express their thoughts in metaphor or to see meanings. In other words, does 2+2=4? Or is 2+2 an example of addition? Both are correct ways of interpreting the data. Remember the story about Sylvia and Tracy? Sylvia walks by the corner of Market Street and Fourth Avenue one morning and sees Tracy standing there with a penguin. Rather amazed, she asks, "Tracy, what are you doing with that penguin?" "I don't know," she answered. "It just wandered up, and now it won't leave. I don't know what to do with it." "Look," said Sylvia, "Why don't you just take it to the zoo?" "That's a great idea," said Tracy. "I think I will." The next day, Sylvia is walking to work again and passes the same corner. There, to her amazement, is Tracy again, standing with the same penguin. "I thought you were going to take that penguin to the zoo," said Sylvia. "I did," Tracy replied. "He liked it so much that today we are going to the theater." Who is the literalist?

Sometimes there are humorous consequences; sometimes the consequences are more profound. One of my clients tells a story about his secretary, an ISFP, that helps to underscore this difference. In her previous company, her supervisor had been transferred and a new section chief had taken over. They had offices across the hallway from one another. This section chief had a supervisor who was suspicious of all new employees who had been transferred from some other part of the organization, and therefore kept close tabs on them until they proved themselves. For the first week that the new section chief was in the organization, his supervisor called the ISFP secretary each day at about 10:00 am and asked if her boss was "there." Each time he called, the answer was the same: "No sir, I'm sorry, he's not here. Would you like him to call you?" By the fifth day, the supervisor was apoplectic and finally blurted out: "What time, pray tell, does your new section chief get into the office?" "Oh," said the secretary, "about 7:00 am each morning." "Well, why is he never there, then, when I call at 10:00 am?" he asked. "Because, sir, his office is across the hall," she replied. What, exactly, does "there" mean? Sometimes, different things for sensors and intuitives.

It is as though the sensor rips the paper off the back of the printer, holds it up, and says, "this is reality; this is what is important." The intuitive, instead, prefers to report on the possibilities inherent in the data and the relationships among the data. My wife will come home from work when the telephone rings. Our sensing son races for the phone, and we hear him say: "Yes, she is." Click—and he hangs up. My wife says, "Honey, who was on the phone?" The ESTP says, "Oh, it was the Chairman; he wanted to know if you were here. I said, yes." He's right, of course, and that drives me nuts.

A few years ago, I came home from a trip to Italy. I had been working in Parma and Rome for about a week, and returned just in time for supper, the first day of school for our fifth grader. I jet-lagged my way out of the limo, walked into our house, and found my family sitting at the table ready for supper. Our ten-year-old ESTP was sitting at the supper table wearing his baseball cap at the table, knowing that his attire was bound to please Pop. You see, wearing a baseball cap at the supper table is a sign of genuine "hickdom" in the Jeffries household. He knows that, hence, the hat! I remained my normally loving, nurturing INTJ self and asked him a question showing my care and concern about his ongoing educational experience. I asked, "Hey, buddy, about how many kids are in your class this year?" I think this shows genuine interest, wouldn't you say?

He looks at me, turns his baseball cap backwards—knowing I really value that appearance—folds his arms across his chest and says, "It's not an 'about' question!" I ask, "What do you mean, it's not an 'about' question?" He replies, "Look, Pop, there are 23 kids in my class." The point is that it's not an "about" question, and when I ask an "about" question to a sensor, it's me who sounds stupid, not him.

Let's think about a business example of the same issue. One of my clients is a large chemical company. The chairman is a sensor. One of his EVP's, running a business out of New Jersey, is an intuitive. In January, the chairman calls the EVP and asks, "Lenny, how many square meters of product did we ship from the Charleston, South Carolina facility in December, last year?" Lenny says, "Half a million square meters." The chairman thanks him and hangs up. It's not two weeks later when the quarterly spread sheets come across the chairman's desk in Pennsylvania, and he sees the figures for December in black and white reporting 497,612 square meters. He's on the telephone not thirty minutes later. "I thought you said half a million." "Yes, that's right," Lenny said. "No, it's not," said the chairman. "Can't I trust you to get anything right? What are you trying to hide in New Jersey?" Trust me, as an intuitive: 497,612—that's half a million! But not for the sensor. We do this kind of thing to ourselves every day. What looks like an ethics issue is often just a different way of seeing reality.

On one occasion, I was working with some American engineers employed by the German Hoechst Corporation. We were doing a start-up venture in Japan. As luck would

27

have it, the Japanese leadership team was comprised entirely of sensors. Now, I do not mean to imply anything about national demographics by this example. But in this case, type was almost monolithic. At the same time, the American team was almost entirely intuitive in make-up. The American team leader would repeatedly ask, "How's the process going?" The Japanese team had no idea how to answer her question, which, by the way, is an intuitive phrasing. But, when I suggested that she ask, "Is the plant working to 85 % efficiency in output?" the sensors replied, "No, we are at 83 % efficiency. We expect to be at 85 % by October 1st." Books like *Kiss, Bow, or Shake Hands* by Morrison, Conaway, and Borden and *Managing Across Borders* by Bartlett and Ghoshal are wonderful additions to our cross-cultural understanding, but they miss critical issues around type that affect every culture.

This need to understand one another's point of view was driven home to me years ago by a close friend who told me a story of her trip to Lanzarote in the Canary Islands. She was on an underground tour exploring some caves when the tour guide beckoned everyone to the edge of a deep crevasse. He asked the group to listen carefully as he dropped a rock into the deep crevasse to attempt to plumb its depth. When they looked down, they all peered into a crevasse that appeared to drop down forever beneath their feet. When the guide dropped the rock, almost immediately there was a splash, and my friend watched as small ripples quickly spread across the surface of a pond, which was almost at their feet. The crevasse was simply the reflection, on an almost perfectly serene surface, of the cavernous heights above them. The tour guide had had a different perception of reality than my friend. Instantly, however, her perception of reality had fallen in line with the tour guide's. That same flash of recognition rarely occurs for us as we attempt to work with others with greatly different perceptions, but something akin can begin as we come to realize that our view is not the only view of reality.

THINKING JUDGMENT VS. FEELING JUDGMENT

Once we have recorded our perceptions, Jung suggests that we have to make some decisions about them. It does not matter how we gathered those perceptions; there is no determining link between perceiving and judging preferences. They are two equally rational decision-making processes—two different ways of arriving at closure. Thinking judgers prefer to judge their perceptions logically and non-personally. These analytical judgers tend to objectify their judging process and arrive at closure in a manner that may seem to those with the opposite preference as cool and somewhat insensitive to human concerns.

Those persons with the opposite preference, those called feeling judgers, prefer to reason about their perceptions more personally—subjectively reflecting on the effect that their perceptions may have on people, relationships, and interpersonal values. Because of their subjectivity, these individuals can often come across to others as more concerned, personally involved, empathetic, and caring than those with a thinking preference.

A couple of cautions are in order when considering the judging function. First, the words thinking and feeling do not mean, in the context of Jungian psychology, what we mean by those words when we use them in our day-by-day speech. They were coined by a German in the early part of the century, and he is dead. So part of our task entails figuring out what this dead German meant by those words many years ago. In the context of the indicator, the word thinking has nothing to do with intelligence (despite what your "T" friends might tell you), and nothing to do with cognitive capability. Similarly, the word feeling has nothing to do with emotions—nothing whatsoever. If you were taught in the past that it did, you were badly taught; there is a lot of bad teaching out there with the Myers-Briggs, as there is with most personality surveys. The words mean other things.

Second, it is critical to realize that each is a rational function. Neither has the corner on making quality decisions; each simply reasons about her or his preferences through different filters. Their mutual rationality is what led Jung to refer to these two as the "rational" functions.

SOME KEY WORDS

Thinking	Feeling
Objective	Subjective
Non-personal	Interpersonal
Cool	Warm
Charity	Harmony
Head	Heart
Analytical	Relational
Sympathy	Empathy
Justice	Mercy
Critique	Compliment

Here's how it might work. Let's say the Director of Human Resources has given you the assignment to arrange a rather elegant dinner welcoming the new director of international marketing for Europe. As a thinking judger—a "T"—you decide to seat people according to a logical method: rank within the organization, Hay level, job assignment, or position. You might even decide to do away with the traditional "pecking order" and simply assign the guests seats alphabetically. That is also a logical approach.

In passing, you mention your plan to your office mate—an "F." She complains that you have missed the point.

30

Supper is a good time to enhance relationships, so your "F" office mate suggests seating people together who rarely have an opportunity to speak with one another because they come from diverse geographical locations. Neither approach is more or less correct, but notice the different way each focuses the decision-making lens.

It is this lens that sometimes brings "T's" and "F's" into conflict. As a "T," I could easily sympathize with the plight of my employees for whom daycare was not just a convenience but a necessity. My "F" colleague, however, did not sympathize with them; he empathized with them. While I sympathized about their circumstances and wanted to help them find suitable facilities, my "F" colleague was there with them, identifying with their needs to such an extent that the need became his as well as theirs: empathy not sympathy.

Once, when working with an INTP plant manager in Portsmouth, Virginia, to implement a teambuilding program within his organization, my "F" colleague and I were out-briefing him regarding a series of interviews we had conducted during the day. We had been aware that the previous week he had received permission from his business director to hire a new technical manager for the plant. He had already decided who the person should be but had been too busy to extend the offer to the person. At the out-briefing, he turned to his director of human resources and said: "I finally got around to offering the job to the person we discussed." As an INTJ, I thought to myself, "Hmm, so the INTP finally 'got around to making the offer,' and there are just seven days until the person he replaces will be gone. We may have an 'NP' leadership problem here." At the same instant, my ENFJ colleague said, "Oh, the poor man. I bet he was dying to find out." In other words, she saw a human relations problem. As a "T," I was more concerned with analyzing the process. As

31

an "F," she was concerned with the needs of that person.

What makes the difference, we really do not know. What research points out, however, is that substantially more men are "T's" and substantially more women are "F's." The general population is split roughly 50 % "T" and 50 % "F." But that is where the similarity ends. About two thirds of all women report feeling preferences, and about two thirds of all men report "T" preferences. What that means is that "T" women and "F" men swim up stream in organizations. "T" women and "F" males each get called a whole variety of unflattering names for doing very well that for which their gender counterparts receive praise.

There is as much confusion within the Myers-Briggs community as without concerning this distinction. Many "F's" who are qualified users of the instrument want to claim values as their special prerogative. I hear "F" after "F" speaking at type conferences and making presentations on psychological type who imply that "F's" are value-centered and "T's" are not. You also hear this mantra repeated in some of the more popular books on type. It is a bias that infects the type community. Both "F's" and "T's" can be value-centered, and each can be value-neutral or worse. "F's" base their values on subjective criteria, and "T's" base their values on more objective criteria. Here is an example that may clarify the difference.

I was talking with some consultants at a Charlotte, North Carolina-based consulting firm about a number of contemporary environmental issues. A few of them discovered that they shared the same view regarding a debate over tuna fishing. Since thousands of dolphins (the mammal, not the food fish) are killed inadvertently each year in the process of commercial tuna fishing, these people had all decided to forego eating tuna as a protest against the inhumane drowning of dolphins that occurred when the nets designed for tuna also snared the dolphins who apparently travel together. These employees, all "F's," requested that the firm take a public stance against the tuna industry. The CEO, a "T," agreed, saying she thought the situation was morally reprehensible. The "F's," two women and one man, were pleasantly surprised by the boss's comments. Only when they began to explore why they had all decided to stop eating tuna, did the sparks begin to fly.

As the female CEO explained, "I have personally decided to stop eating tuna because the current practice by many tuna wholesalers encourages the mass destruction of this precious natural resource as a consequence of their current fishing methods. We are in danger of losing a natural resource, without which our planet would be a poorer place." As another "T," I was surprised by her position but at the same time fairly impressed by her thoughtfulness, zeal, commitment, and sympathetic understanding of the dolphins' plight. The "F's" were appalled!

As they explained it, "Sure, we're in danger of losing a precious, irreplaceable resource, but the real agony is that mammals, just like us, other animals that give birth to live, air-breathing young are being smothered under tuna nets just to line the fishermen's pockets with more money. It's horrible! I can almost feel myself being dragged down with them, struggling for my last breath, suffocating. God, I feel for them! They are my brothers; they are me. Think of all the stories you have heard of dolphins saving people's lives. How can we stand by and watch them suffer?" As an INTJ, I think they are nuts! Where did all that come from, I wonder to myself? The answer is, it came from their empathy for others and their willingness always to "walk a mile in their brothers' (or, in this case, their fellow mammals') moccasins." As a "T," I don't have that desire.

33

Heck, I'd sell their moccasins on E-Bay for a profit.

At least, in that example, the two sides agreed on the solution. They just had vastly different ways of getting there. That is not usually the case. Sometimes it is the MEANS that frustrate people; other times it is the ENDS themselves.

I was with two friends in Fairfax, Virginia in the 1990's shortly after a terrible earthquake had struck northern Iran. The wife, an ENFJ, had just read in *The Washington Post* that over 40,000 people had been killed. She was literally sobbing as she told her INTP husband, an army helicopter pilot stationed at the Pentagon, about the tragedy. She was trying to express her horror, her sense of loss, her anguish over all those who had been killed, and the pain she felt for their loved ones. Dan tried to commiserate with her and express his equal concern over the event and said warmly and lovingly, "Try to think of it this way, Maureen. One day 40,000 people go to a baseball game, but they just don't come back." See any difference here? Don't come back, indeed!

The "F" was dumbstruck by what appeared to be the "T's" indifference to human life. The "T" was perplexed by his partner's inability to see his deep remorse. It is often a matter of attachment or detachment. The "T" has a preference for dealing with such incidents in a more detached fashion, as though the process took place in a small bubble out in the air, like the bubbles used to indicate a dialogue in a cartoon strip. The "F" takes that same bubble and tucks it inside and thinks in terms of I, me, you, and us. That is the critical "T-F" difference, and it is a gulf not easily bridged.

This is a difference that is far too easy to blame on gender.

34

Deborah Tannen's *You Just Don't Understand: Women and Men in Conversation* and John Gray's *Men are From Mars, Women are From Venus* try to sensitize us to male and female communication patterns. You can take their books and virtually each time the authors use the words "male" and "female" substitute the words "thinking judgers" and "feeling judgers." Sadly, because of the gender bias on this dimension, the authors are both wrong, at least one third of the time. They also attack the wrong problem.

Sadly, we often don't even know when we have offended someone along this dimension. Several years ago when Governor Dukakis was running for president against the elder George Bush, there was a "T-F" confrontation in the third presidential debate that ruined Dukakis's chances for higher office. During the debate, Bernard Shaw asked Dukakis a very controversial question: "Governor, given your personal stance on capital punishment (he was adamantly opposed to it), what would you want done if your own wife were raped and murdered?" Dukakis, a "T" (actually an INTJ), gave this three and a half minute answer, "Well, Bernie, as you know, I have always been ethically opposed...blah, blah, blah," and not once mentioned his wife, Kitty, by name. The next day he lost fourteen points in the national polling and eventually lost the election. America has voted for "F" presidents, or at least those who can fake a good "F" mask, every single time since Richard Nixon. Dukakis's strength was his "T." It was what had enabled him to create the Massachusetts Miracle—the ability to make the calm, cool decision, unruffled by the emotions of the moment. His very strength was his undoing. His is a cautionary tale for all of us. In every case, our strength maximized can become our greatest liability.

Our preferences become so much a part of our personality, so "normal," that the words are out of our mouths and

35

feelings are bruised before we know it. About a year ago, I was sitting in a friend's house in St. Nicolas, Belgium, having a friendly chat after a delightful wild game dinner. Off to the side of the sitting room was a lovely, ivory and fruitwood inlaid antique sideboard. One of my associates, a "T," had just returned from working with a financial team in southern Russia. In less than glowing terms, he was describing the Spartan living conditions in his hotel. At one point he said, "and the furniture, you can't believe how wretched it was. It was just a bunch of old, ugly uncomfortable junk, kinda like that thing over there." And, of course, he was pointing to the antique sideboard, our hostess's prized heirloom. I chanced to catch the eye of my "F" partner, and we could barely contain ourselves. The "T" had no idea—until our hostess threw a plate of croissants at him—that he had said anything untoward.

It was almost as bad as the "F" who asks her lover, "Why don't you ever tell me you love me any more?" The "T" asks, "Didn't I tell you I loved you when I married you?" "Yes, yes!" she squeals. "If anything changes," he says romantically, "I'll let you know!"

EXTRAVERSION VS. INTROVERSION

Once a person's preferences for the modes of perception and judgment have been decided, he or she has declared what Jung referred to as the two fundamental forms of mental functioning. People do it; animals do it. I have some weird friends who teach on university faculties who think plants do it. But I know you do it. You gather perceptions ("S" or "N") and you judge them ("T" or "F"). Once I know what you prefer, your team prefers, or your organization prefers, there is nothing we cannot assist you to do better, safer, faster, with higher quality, and with greater productivity. That is the brilliance of the indicator and the power of our business models.

The next distinction to discover is the one that Jung, in

the early part of his career, saw as the most important distinction—that between extraversion and introversion. The difficulty here, as with the words feeling and thinking, is that the words do not mean, in the context Jung developed them, what we often mean by these words when we use them in our general conversation. An extravert is not necessarily loud and talkative, and an introvert is not necessarily shy and withdrawn. Were I writing the indicator, I would select different words, but we are stuck with these words because Jung coined them to describe the difference. As Isabel reminded us, extraverts are people whose interests run to the external world of people and things; whereas, introverts are those whose interests run to the internal world of ideas and concepts.

SOME KEY WORDS

Extraverts	Introverts
Gregarious	Demurring
Breadth	Depth
Action	Reflection
Sociable	Reserved
Expressive	Reticent
External	Internal
Many	Few
Open	Private
Outward Focus	Inward Focus
Interaction	Concentration
People	Privacy

Too often this difference is treated as merely a difference in noise level; the distinction, however, is far richer. I have been seated next to introverts on airplane trips who talked my ear off the entire trip. We discussed the events of September 11, 2001, the second Bush presidency, Afghanistan, the current problems in the Middle East, the Clinton Administration vendetta against Microsoft, David

Letterman's humor, the introduction of the Euro, and the tech wreck of the dotcoms. Five hours later when our plane sets down in San Diego, I will not know the person's name or where she is from. Those topics have never come up. We have discussed many things, but nothing about the introvert, herself. On the other hand, I can sit next to a very quiet extravert and not speak a word for four hours, but in the last fifteen minutes before landing in Houston, Texas learn that his marriage is in trouble, his son is gay, his daughter is doing drugs, he made $2 million on Enron stock, and he has gas: things no introvert would tell you if they had known you for three years. In fact, and you have experienced this phenomenon yourself, sometimes extraverts will tell you things you just know you should not know.

This dilemma is what Isabel and her mother had in mind when they referred to the Extravert—Introvert distinction as being the "arena of energy flow." What charges up and energizes one, drains the other. If an extravert has a very busy day, one telephone call after another, one teleconference, cold call, luncheon, and team meeting after the other, the "E" can come home tired, but so full of potential energy she can't wait to tell you about her day. She has to do a data dump or explode. Put an introvert in the same kind of "hectic" day and by 2:00 pm her door, which is usually partially closed, is shut. The "I" just wants to get in her car and drive home, hoping to goodness that you are not there when she arrives. Then someone suggests the "I" carpool and take a friend. "Sure! Just what I need!"

In the workplace, introverts can sometimes be seen as not being very good team players. Let's say I am an extravert and have a conversation with my supervisor in her office. We chat for about an hour behind the closed door. When I return to my desk to work, it occurs to me that I should let Molly know what the boss and I discussed, so I give her a call. Fifteen minutes later I meet Leshawn at the coffee pot and discuss with him part of the conversation I had with our mutual boss. Back in the office, I e-mail Perry and Estevan some thoughts about the conversation I had with my supervisor and copy Len Ho, Marty, and Stephan so they aren't out of the loop. All that is natural for the extravert. If I am an "E" I tend to have a breadth of relationships and keep them involved in my life whether they want it or not.

If I, as an introvert, have that same conversation with my supervisor, I will most likely return to my desk and go back to work. I say nothing to anyone, because it is none of their business. Rest assured that those who need to know will eventually be informed; it just is not a priority. Guaranteed, within thirty minutes the extraverts will be meeting at the water fountain asking, "What's up? Did he say anything to you?" "No, how about you?" "Not me. Maybe he's out of here." "No, he just always has a hidden agenda."

The bias against introversion in our culture all goes back to high school. Some teacher said to you, "In this class, this semester, 20 % of your grade is based on—class participation." With that simple phrase, the teacher, unless he or she is very savvy, has just thrown the gauntlet to the extraverted child and begun to disadvantage the Introvert. When the teacher asks, "Kids, which countries border on Turkey?" you can spot the extraverts in a heartbeat: "OOOh, I've got it, Iran, Iraq, Russia;" "No, over here, I know them, there is Greece and Germany," "No, she's wrong …" and the extraverts literally start talking their way back to the answer.

As an Introvert, I hated them back then. Now I know why. Extraverts always seemed to know where the answer was. It was out "there" somewhere, and all they had to do to find it was to start their mouths moving until they located it. The introvert also knows where the answer is; it is inside, and so the introvert goes inside to find it. In business meetings, it is the extravert who runs the meetings. "Let's do some brainstorming." So the "E's" are out there offering one idea after another. Forty-five minutes into the meeting, the introvert raises her hand and says, "You know, I've been thinking." "Oh, really?" rejoins the extravert. "Didn't know you were here. Thanks for finally playing."

From the introvert's perspective, thank goodness for e-mail. I can talk to anyone, on my terms, and not have to see them. Hallelujah! In fact, if I am smart and savvy, I can wait until the person is not in the office and e-mail them then. That way I never have to talk to them. On the other hand, watch when you get an e-mail from an extravert. You open the e-mail, and twenty minutes later the extravert is on the telephone, "Hey, did you get my e-mail? Want to talk about it?" What charges up one, drains the other.

In the workplace, we each disadvantage the other. If you are an extravert, you can disadvantage your introverted co-workers by noise level and physical presence. That's right, just being there ticks them off. Let's say the intro-vert is working at his desk. He hears this ball of noise coming down the hallway. Curiously, he gets up, opens his door—forget the "open door policy," introverts do their best work behind closed doors—and asks, "What's so exciting? What's all the noise?" The extravert responds by saying, "I was just thinking, that's all." "Well, if you were just thinking," asks the introvert, "Why were your lips moving?" And some of you know why, don't you? Some extraverts have to hear themselves say something to know what they think. Introverts wouldn't think of saying something until they have thought it through.

Then they respond.

And then there is simple "physical presence." The "E" walks in to the "I's" office and stands next to her. The longer the "E" is there, the closer she will get. Eventually, the "E" will have to touch. Extraverts cannot not touch. They sit on your desk, unconsciously slide your things off to the side, and engage you in conversation about your thoughts about the new dress code for the office. And the "I" is groaning: "Just get them out of here!"

Likewise, if you are an introvert, you can disadvantage your extraverted colleagues in at least two ways, as well. First of all, "E's" need to know what the "I's" are think-ing. And just being who we are, we do not share very much. The extravert has to pull it out of us bit by bit. It is as though we have some "hidden agenda." Furthermore, extraverts need to be able to bounce some thoughts off the introvert and get some feedback. That's how they learn. The "I's" give really exciting feedback like, "Hmm, ooh, ah." That is not very illuminating feedback for the extravert. We each disadvantage the other, day by day.

There are often some humorous outcomes to this pair of preferences. My father-in-law is an extravert (ESFP). He has spent a lifetime helping people: in the army, as a para-medic, police officer, owner of an ambulance service in the back woods of Wisconsin, mechanic, city coroner, and a host of other activites we associate with an SP's approach to life. Everywhere he has gone, people have known "Jack." He makes friends everywhere and doesn't have to try. He strikes up conversations with people everywhere about everything. What always amazes my family and me is that others seem to like it.

Several years ago, my introverted wife, introverted mother-in-law, and extraverted father-in-law were walking into a Wendy's in Charlotte, North Carlolina. Parked out front was a classic, high handlebar Harley Hog. Getting off the bike was your stereotype of a Harley biker–very large, very sweaty, bald in front and ponytail in back, very hairy, heavily inked, wearing the colors of a notorious biker gang–the Outlaws. In short, he was the kind of guy most middleclass Americans cross the street to avoid.

Jack, who has always loved things mechanical and always wished he could have afforded a Harley, yells at the guy and says: "If I had that there bike, and you had a feather up you're a__, we'd both be tickled!" My wife dropped her jaw and prepared to run, my mother-in-law was mortified, and both thought they were all dead. The biker laughed and said "right on Dude," and Jack smiled, just being his friendly self. A flaming extravert having a casual afternoon off, meeting a new friend.

JUDGING VS. PERCEIVING

The last choice is the pair that Isabel and Kathy added to Jung's typology. They believed they saw it implicit in Jung's writings, but the dichotomy is not stated explicitly. They added this dimension so we would have a way of understanding which function we externalize and which one we internalize in our actions day-by-day. "J's" extravert their judging function, and "P's" extravert their perceiving function.

This is the pair of preferences that is an ongoing lesson in organizational civics; it can be quick to breed ill will and disharmony in organizations. The choice is that between ordering and structuring experiences or going with the flow and adapting to what comes along. The person with a preference for judging prefers order and structure. The person with a preference for perceiving has a passion for adaptability.

SOME KEY WORDS

Judging	Perceiving
Closed	Open
Structure	Adapt
Decisive	Tentative
Planned	Spontaneous
Control	Experience
Order	Randomness
Plan	Wait and See
Regulate	Flow
Schedule	Spontaneity
Deadlines	Discoveries
Organized	Flexible

This is often the easiest preference to see in others because we have such unflattering terms with which to describe them. The "J" looks at the "P" and sees someone they expect to be late for church, be late for meetings, sit at messy desks, and start projects at the last minute. "J's" call them flaky. "P's," on the other hand, see "J's" as rigid, arbitrary, and anal retentive. All it has to do with is how much order and structure we like in our lives.

"P's" tend to exasperate "J's" with their bottomless supply of new suggestions or alternative ways of completing a project. Likewise, "J's" can perplex "P's" with their passion for order, structure, and closure. If we are in the same meeting with a planned completion time of 2:30 pm, rest assured that by 2:15 pm, the "J's" will be summarizing the discussion, boiling it down to three talking points and two action items with a PPR assigned for each action item. With five minutes left in the meeting, the "P" is likely to say something like, "You know, we haven't even looked at the data from Singapore yet." The meeting doesn't end on time but goes for fifty minutes longer than planned. You can watch the "J's" knuckles turning white, their whole schedule is screwed up, they need another list, and the "P's" have just kept you from making a sixty-five thousand dollar mistake. Which is why "J's" and "P's" desperately need each other. "E's" and "I's," "S's" and "N's," "T's" and "F's," and "J's" and "P's" all need each other; that's the point. I have one preference; you have the opposite. Together, we are usually better off.

Individually, and collectively, we always run the risk of getting blindsided around our non-preferences. That is why life involves a lifetime of learning about how to understand and use our non-preferences.

QUESTIONS & ANSWERS

QUESTION 1
What is the origin of our preferences?

Schools of developmental psychology too often fall into warring camps with one of two operating premises: nature or nurture. The distinction, first formulated by the Greeks over two millennia ago, has divided any number of disciplines over the years. At the simplest level, those who hold to the former see genetics as the factor primarily responsible for human characteristics. Those who hold to the latter see environment as the factor most responsible. We can find practitioners of type theory in each camp. That distinction is complicated by the fact that Jungians can also be found in either camp.

As I read Jung's writings in the original German, however, it becomes clear that Jung himself ascribed our traits to genetics. In other words, according to Jung, we are born with our preferences. He couldn't prove that thesis any more than Plato could have proved to his colleagues in Athens centuries earlier that we all had certain innate philosophical thought forms he called "ideals" or "forms," but Jung was convinced our preferences were innate. While type theory begins with Jung, there is not a perfect congruence. Clearly, our preferences are also shaped, molded, reinforced, or restricted by our environment, friends, family, religious training, jobs, and a myriad of other factors that help to develop us as unique individuals.

I readily admit, as soon as someone tells me I am biologically scripted to do anything, I want to smack him. Philosophically, religiously, and socially, I see myself as a human version of a free electron, some would say a free radical, fully capable of charting my course, independent of biological loading. Unfortunately, the data over the years shows me that I am wrong. It looks like our preferences are biologically determined. Like Jung, I can't prove it, but I can offer a couple pieces of anecdotal evidence.

One of our research groups with which I enjoy working is comprised entirely of identical twins. This group takes care of the "nature" premise, because they have each come from the same egg. When the egg splits and pops out two zygotes, each has 100 % of the DNA and RNA coding of the other—nature at its best. Some of these pairs came from the Minnesota Twins study, some from our work in Asia and Latin America, some come from some of the war-torn countries of the former Yugoslavia and parts of Bosnia, some from the African continent, and a few have come from participants in our seminars in the United States as well as other parts of the world.

To add the variable of "nurture," we look just at identical twins that have been separated at birth—usually the same day—and raised separately in different families, different cultures, and often in different countries. So far we have identified 148 sets of identical twins, who, the day of birth, were separated and raised separately. The research question we posed was, is there some degree of "fixed action patterns," as biologists describe them? In less arcane speech, would there be a relationship between the separated twins? Would they tend to be type alike or typologically different?

When all the twin pairs completed the indicator, fourteen in French, thirteen in German, nine in Spanish, four with a research version in Portuguese, nine in Chinese, two in

Italian, and the rest with the American version, the results were remarkable. Of the one hundred forty-eight sets of identical twins, one hundred thirty-seven sets reported the same four preferences. It is admittedly a small sample, but it is a statistically significant one. *It looks like we are hard wired.* Most biologists would have a fit at my suggesting that conclusion, but most psychologists would find the conclusion intriguing. I, as an engineer, find the data compelling! If you happen to be half of a matched set who was separated from your sibling at birth, I would love to hear from you.

Dr. Walter Lowen's research in *Dichotomies of the Mind* also fascinates me. If he is correct that "SF," "ST," "NF," and "NT" each resides on a specific level of the cerebral cortex, the thesis forms an exciting starting point for plotting the type geography of the brain. Add to that the possibility that the front (cerebral) part of the brain is extraverted and the rear (limbic) part of the brain, where all new data enters, is introverted and posit further that the left hemisphere (that part of the brain we always saw as linear, final, and sequential) is "J," and the right hemisphere (that part we traditionally associated with musical, creative, and adaptive) is "P," and we get some interesting possibilities.

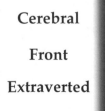 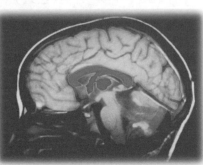

Cerebral

Front

Extraverted

Limbic

Rear

Introverted

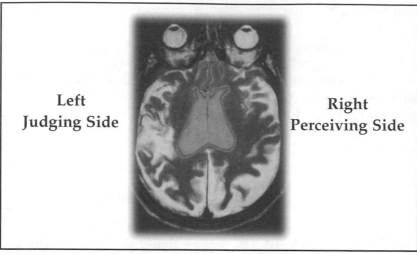

The map would reflect sixteen nodal ganglia, each representing one of the sixteen types, which develop in a predictable order. First developed is right cerebral, then right limbic, then left cerebral then left limbic, and so on for each of the four levels of the cerebral cortex moving from the inside out.

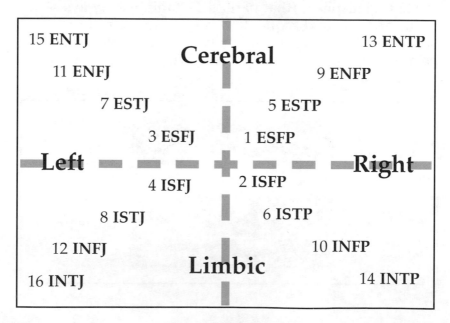

Howard Grant's theory of type development becomes more powerful, and the possibilities for the medical arts become fascinating if not frightening. Just think, if this mapping is correct, if I wanted an ENTJ, theoretically I could make one, chemically, surgically, or electronically. Concomitantly, if I didn't want those preferences, I could destroy them the same way. Hmmm. We call that technology eugenics, and several years ago we had to destroy a regime that abused it.

Two decades from now, we will probably have a great more certainty than today about where our INTJ or ESTP or ISFJ originates. The untangling of the human genome holds the key to reeducating ourselves about a multitude of issues regarding origins and transferences. What we understand about human personality today may be completely overturned by that weird science. But for today we would have to admit that type is a reflection of both nature and nurture. Both play a role in who we see ourselves to be and what we prefer. But the data clearly leans heavily in the direction of nature. I may not like it, but it looks like type is biologically driven. As Kevin Soden, a physician buddy of mine, puts it, "genetics loads the gun, but environment pulls the trigger."

QUESTION 2
How does "True Type" differ from my "Myers-Briggs Type"?

This distinction is a critical one both for practitioners of type as well as those completing the survey. In short, the four preferences you report on the indicator may indicate how you see yourself or how you are presently acting, but they may or may not be your "true type." You must be the one to make that decision, not a consultant or presenter. I always shudder when clients tell me that they reported four preferences on the indicator, but the person making the presentation on the results said they were actually four different preferences. The theory holds that each of us has a "true type." Whether or not the MBTI® reflects that type at any one taking is, to a certain extent, up for grabs, depending on the scientific credibility of the form used, and the circumstances, frame of mind, and "honesty" of the person taking the indicator.

There are several reasons why individuals may misreport themselves. Perhaps they find themselves in jobs where a certain style of behavior is expected and maybe even rewarded. Perhaps they have heard just enough about type from others to believe that a certain type is "better" for a job than others. For example, for a few years I was an adjunct faculty member in the graduate education school of Old Dominion University, in Norfolk, Virginia. One semester I guest taught a course for about thirty teachers, all of whom were aspiring candidates for jobs as guidance counselors. The professor who normally taught this course was the head guidance counselor for the City of Norfolk public school system. As part of the program, the graduate students all completed the MBTI®. One of the individuals, by virtue of her position in the school system, obtained access to a set of scoring keys and, prior to handing in her answer sheet to me, scored her answer sheet herself and discovered she had picked INTP. This was her true type, but having heard or read, somewhere, that the typical type for high school guidance directors was ESFJ, she went back and redid her answers, erasing almost every one and marking the opposite response, so that she would come out ESFJ when I tallied her responses. She did not want to appear to be the "wrong type" to her professor who would be making hiring decisions after the students received their degrees. A simple, but not infrequent, misunderstanding of how the results might be used, had caused this problem.

Sad to say, similar dilemmas face people in many professions. We often hear subtly or more overtly, "shape up or ship out!" Given all the changes swirling around us today, businesses desperately need people bringing their true types to the job every day. Masks are fine, even healthy as we change behaviors frequently to meet different needs. But when the person becomes the mask is when we find ourselves in a position that the French philosopher Jean Paul Sartre would have called many years ago, "inauthenticity." American variations of that state run the gauntlet from a nerdish Al Gore trying to dress and act like an alpha male to the potential for a scenario like a Columbine massacre.

Family pressures to conform can likewise discourage individuals from reporting honest "preferences" on the indicator. Our research for years has shown, for example, a disproportionate number (as would be expected in the general population) of _NFP children in military families, where the predominant uniformed parent is ISTJ and ESTJ and the other parent is ESFJ or ISFJ. Is the child's reported type an indication of rebellion, the desire to provide something different from what they see as the norm, the need for flexibility in an otherwise rigid system, the need to be able to respond to frequent moves, or "true type"? We just don't know. The individual is the final arbiter.

In families of corporate executives, physicians, and politicians, where the spousal types are much the same as above, we see much the same kind of data. Over the years the numbers have become quite significant. What we find specifically is that in a sample of 18,500 families (military and corporate combined) where one or more of the parents is a "TJ" (ISTJ, ESTJ, INTJ, and ENTJ), children tend to report "_NFP" as preferences 49 % of the time. We would expect to find such preferences only in approximately 6 % of the general population. Misreporting our types—what is called "falsification of type" (See Question

51

23)—is a real phenomenon, and we who are "TJ" parents are often responsible for it. In many cases, we are playing the "shape up or ship out" game with our kids, and the consequences can be deadly.

Of course there are other reasons as well that individuals may misreport their types. These reasons range from being under stress to misunderstanding the questions or the words on the indicator. There are also those who may have been culturally, socially, or linguistically disadvantaged and those whose level of education is inadequate to respond to the questions. Those for whom English is a second language, those from non-white, non-male groups, or those people just enjoying normal developmental changes may likewise misreport themselves. The burden is on the consultant, however, to ensure that clients do not assume that the indicator is telling them their type. Each individual must decide for himself or herself. The language we should use in reporting a person's type, therefore, should be something like, "When you completed the indicator, you reported yourself as...."

QUESTION 3
Which version of the indicator should I take?

Once upon a time, this was a rather easy question to answer. At any one time there was one "Authorized Version." Today, if you check with the publisher of the MBTI®, Consulting Psychologists Press, they will dazzle you with language around Step I, Step II, and Step III approaches to personality type. By step I, they mean taking the indicator and getting four letters back—your preferences, or your four letter type. Step II parses your type into twenty subscales to help you understand some subtleties of your preferences. Step III adds seven "comfort-discomfort scales" (See Question 61).

The version they recommend for Step I is the current form

they call the authorized one—form M. If you talk with one of the hundreds of consultants who actually use the indicator for a myriad of personal and organizational issues, they will usually tell you which form they currently use; that will be form G, K, or M (See Question 61). Usually those forms will have to be mailed out from a qualified user of the form or in some rare cases (our company being one), you can take the indicator on line.

Sometimes people have taken the Keirsey Sorter (the 70-question survey in *Please Understand Me* or available on line) and believe they have completed the MBTI®. They have not. The Sorter is an interesting form that does not have the psychometric credibility of the indicator. Because the author, David Keirsey, is a brilliant researcher and prolific writer on type-related subjects, the form will usually work, if a person's preferences are very clear. If one's preferences are slight or moderate, the form can be as wrong as all four letters. It is not an authorized version of the indicator, however brilliantly designed it might be, and should not be advertised as such.

I believe that the best form to take currently is form G, which has been the Authorized Version for over a decade. *If you complete the MBTI® with Executive Strategies International, Inc., you will take form G* into the foreseeable future. We are clearly spitting into the wind on this issue, because the publisher is free to make any claims they want for the new form. If they so desire, they could pull form G off the market tomorrow, and we would probably be constrained to use form M. Ethically, however, we would be remiss if we did not state our objection to the new form and the process used to develop it. We do not believe the publisher has made a case for changing the form or for adding Step II or Step III approaches (See Question 61). Anything they allege that Steps II and III accomplish, we can do with our in-depth approach to Form G.

QUESTION 4
How reliable are my results?

Usually when people ask this question they are asking whether or not they can trust their results to reflect their true personalities and behaviors. They are not, in other words, really asking about statistical "reliability." So it is best to press them about what they are really asking. If they want to know to what extent the indicator really measures those things it claims to measure, they are concerned with *validity*, or the degree to which inferences about the results can be supported by evidence.

Researchers traditionally discuss statistical validity in terms of criterion-related, content-related, and construct-related forms of evidence. Most users of the indicator need not worry about such fine distinctions because the validation has already been done for them in the appropriate *Manual* corresponding to the version of the indicator being used. Forms F and G, which are the ones used most frequently over the last 20 years, are described in the 1985 *Manual* authored by Myers and McCaulley. Form M's psychometric characteristics are described in the 1998 *Manual* authored by Myers, McCaulley, Quenk, and Hammer.

If by "reliability" you mean "statistical reliability" the answer is slightly different. The question really is what the likelihood is that you will replicate your results on retake—in short, take-retake reliability. The reliability of the results depends on several things (gender, age, education, achievement level, and all those issues discussed in Question 2). It also depends on the strength of the individual preferences—the clearer the preference, the higher the reliability. The consensus among professionals is that any personality indicator should be at least 70 % or higher to be considered reliable. The MBTI® more than fills that bill. Indeed, it is much more reliable than the Firo instruments or the MMPI.

Taking all things into consideration, one can see that the MBTI® is about 85 % reliable—that is impressively high reliability. If, however, you are accustomed to working with such data, you know that 85 % is a rather slippery number. Actually, reliability depends on the numerical strength of the individual preference. On forms F, G, and K, should the preference strength be 1-15, reliability of that particular preference drops to about 70 %. One may change that preference on retake, about 30 % of the time. If a preference strength is between 17-29, then take-retake reliability jumps up to about 86 %, and that preference is likely to change on retake no more than 14 % of the time. But, if a preference strength is over 31… I think it is safe to get the tattoo tonight. The likelihood of changing that preference is in the single digits. All that is is a numerical way of saying "the clearer your preferences, the clearer your preferences," but engineers love those numbers—don't you? Reliability of form M (and hence form Q as well) can be found in the section on "Research" in the 1998 *Manual*. The researchers' claim is that take-retake "reliability for form M is higher than for form G." I remain quite skeptical but will let you be the final arbiter, until we have more data developed by the next edition of this book.

QUESTION 5
If my colleague and I are the same type, why are we so different?

This question, for me, highlights one of the exciting attributes of type theory. Type does not restrict us or demand that we perform in prescribed ways. While a knowledge of type can give us an understanding of predictable differences in individuals and, therefore, allow us to deal with those differences in a more constructive way, it in no way determines our behavior. It simply helps us to see that what might appear to be mere chance variation in human behavior, is, in actuality, the result of predictable preferences rooted deep in the psyche.

Once you know that Bill Jeffries is an INTJ, you do not know precisely how I will act at any given time. What you do know is that when my personality was in the process of forming I picked Yankee Stadium not Shea Stadium. But once I'm in the ballpark, there are about 56,000 seats for me to move among. And that stadium is always under reconstruction. Far from boxing us in, type theory gives us a chance to deal with diversity in the workplace in a much more productive way, truly cherishing our differences for the strengths they bring. Each person is unique, despite his or her preferences.

I enjoy having participants with the same preferences meet and discuss their preferences with one another; this can be a very informative process. Of course you are going to feel at home with those of like type; there will be similar ways of dealing with the world, and frequently it is like "coming home." Often, however, the insights we gain are around differences—sometimes slight, sometimes substantial. Such a process helps individuals understand the nonrestrictive nature of their preferences.

Furthermore, you may be different from colleagues of the same psychological type for reasons that type offers no answer. No paper-and-pen indicator, however well conceived and normed, can sum up human personality. Those of us who appreciate so much the work that Katharine Briggs and Isabel Briggs Myers did to bring the indicator into being sometimes have a hard time admitting this fact, but *type doesn't explain everything.* Human personality is far too rich. If personality were to be illustrated by an iceberg, then perhaps type is the rather substantial tip. But there is much more below the surface than there is above.

Type development and clarity of a person's preferences also play important roles in explaining why two people of the same type may be very different in behavior or appearance. I believe it was Isabel who said something like, "Every ESTJ is like *every* other ESTJ, like *some* other ESTJ's, and like *no* other ESTJ you may ever have met." Even if the story is apocryphal, the sentiment is true. An INFP with preference strengths on form G of I-1, N-3, F-5, & P-3 is behaviorally a very different person than an INFP with preference strengths of I-55, N-49, F-31, & P-59. In fact, a person with very clear INFP preferences may well experience an INFP colleague with less clear preferences as more of an "E," "S," "T," or "J." What we observe as preferences is often a matter of degree. This is partially the reason why it is often difficult to guess the type of a loved one. We see that person in comparison to ourselves.

Similarly, if a person has achieved some degree of good type development (see Question 24), he or she has learned when to use the appropriate function, whether favored or not. For instance, as a golfer, I may prefer using my driver to the other clubs. But even though it is my preferred club, I'm a stupid golfer if I try to putt with it. It's just an analogy to be sure, but it is an apt analogy to type. What I want, if I'm a well-developed golfer, is a bag of eight to sixteen clubs from which I can choose depending on the shot. Making that choice does not naysay the fact that I have a favorite; sometimes, to be pragmatic, I must use a non-preferred club. When individuals have achieved some level of good type development, they occasionally use their nonpreferences with some skill. Nevertheless, their behavior at these times may be interpreted by others as running counter to type.

Forms K and M may provide some additional insights as well. When one looks at the twenty subscales of the Expanded Profile report (See Question 61), the diversity, even among persons with the same four preferences, can be highlighted. For my money, the jury is still out on the long-term credibility of both the Expanded Profile (EP) and the Expanded Interpretive Report (EIR) available through CPP software, but the differences sometimes highlighted by the subscales are, at least, interesting.

QUESTION 6
Can I change my type?

A lot depends on what you mean by "type." The theory says there is a true type for each individual. If you are asking about this type, then the answer is *no; your type does not change.* If you mean, can my reported type change, that is an altogether different issue. Whether or not at any time the indicator picks up the true type is to some extent up for grabs, depending on the scientific credibility of the form (see Question 2), how you chose to address the question when you filled out the form, and what you were going through at the time. Clearly there are some things that can skew our reported type.

Stress, for example, may skew how you reported your preferences. Not, "oops, I dropped my pen" kind of stress; I mean major stress. Let's say you are in the family car on a Sunday afternoon taking a nice drive on the interstate, and your BMW's car horn gets stuck behind 45 Hell's Angels. That kind of stress can skew your preferences. Your five year-old son has a strange rash and a temperature of 105 degrees, Mom checks into a nursing home for the first time, your 26 year-old daughter moves back in with her three kids, while you are driving through the woods at night, Bambi drapes herself across the hood of your Lexus—those experiences can skew your results on the Myers-Briggs. Not unusually, when a person goes though a divorce or separation, the "T-F" line goes crazy for a while. The "F" who feels he or she has been used or taken advantage of suddenly can get very cool and analytical ("T")—"they are not going to get me again!" Similarly, the "T" who goes through a divorce can think, "I probably caused it. My cool, detached style probably did it." That person can get very "F" for a time period while she or he tries to sort out the future (See Question 34).

Often what this question is attempting to probe, however, is the differences in themselves that people see as they mature. Clearly, we do change, we do develop as we go through life, but those changes are more a reflection of our types than they are changes in our types. At a younger age, our preferences tend not to be all that clear. They are there and influential, but they are not developed. Usually, the older we get, the clearer our preferences become. This clarity is often reflected in the numbers associated with the preferences. The theory says we have a type, and if we have accurately identified that type, it does not change.

QUESTION 7
I am a very different person at home from the person I am on the job. How does type theory account for that?

This is a common observation that often arises. Sometimes the question is raised because the individual has not received the proper directions for filling out the MBTI®. The frame of reference an individual uses to answer the questions can color some responses. Unfortunately the directions on the answer sheet are not as clear as they could be. I routinely hand out a supplemental instruction sheet that gives clearer instructions for completing the form than those the publisher includes on the booklet. The point to keep in mind is that the MBTI® is a *preference* indicator based on theory, not behavior. Yet the directions tell us to answer the questions "the way you more often feel or act." The directions seem to tell the respondent to answer behaviorally.

I prefer to be clearer about the purpose of the form and suggest that the client answer all questions with the frame of reference, "Given the best of all possible circumstances, what would you prefer to do, how would you prefer to act, which word appeals more to you?" By preference, I do not mean wishful thinking—"Oh, I wish I could…." I mean, what really runs your ship, what gives you greatest interest or pleasure. With this frame of reference, then, the client has a greater chance of registering consistent preferences, regardless of the setting.

I tend to think about the difference between our behaviors in different environments as analogous to wearing a variety of masks. We pop masks off and on according to the needs of the moment. This idea is analogous to Blanchard's notion of Situational Leadership. When I consult on business high performance, strategy, or new business development or when I coach a senior executive, I wear my true type mask of INTJ. It is I, others recognize me, and it comes across as genuine. I can act other ways, but these four preferences are my long suit.

When I make presentations to a large audience, I change the mask to win the group over and to meet their needs. I am always much more animated and extraverted than is normal for me, but my energy helps to energize the group. I cite data after data and show numerous view-graphs, PowerPoint slides or flip charts to register the content of the presentation in the minds of participants, who are usually predominantly sensing. I come across as very feeling in my understanding of human potential and nuance, and I am continually open to change—I need to go with the audience. In short, my associates tell me that I train as an ESFP. It is the mask I wear.

But there are some other interesting offshoots from this question. Sometimes, sitting in the office filling out the indicator, you may register a set of preferences that differs from the preferences you register when filling out the form while sitting at home. You may be tempted to say, "See, I really am a different person at home from the one I am at work. At work I'm hard charging, bottom-line-oriented, and maybe a little rigid. But I have to be; that's the nature of the job. But at home, I'm a kinder and gentler person, more open to feedback and the concerns of my family. I am really kind of a people person."

Well, as in any business, the customer may be right. But more often than not, if people report their types one way on the job and another way at home, they are just fooling themselves. When such a situation arises, we often allow the person to take the survey in two locations. So, they take it at work sitting behind their desk and again at home on the back porch with a Diet Coke in their hand. When we do this, 14 % of the time a person reports one or more preferences different between the two locations. Then for an honesty check, we give the indicator to a person to fill out on how he or she sees their partner at home. When we do, the result is routinely the same as the one the participant reported on the job.

In our company sample of 39,500 couples who have attended various workshops we sponsor and call themselves "good relationships," 89 % of the time the person at home sees their partner the same as the individual saw himself of herself on the job. In other words, we are very successful in fooling ourselves into thinking that we have dropped a lot more at the office than we have. The family simply does not see us the way we think we are behaving. That misconception can be crucial information for us to know. At home, I see myself as a kinder and gentler Bill. My kids give me different feedback.

QUESTION 8
Is type related to horoscope?

Depending on your philosophical perspective regarding astrology, I could have good news or bad news for you. The informal comparisons that people tell me they have done—none very rigorous—point to there being no correlation between a person's horoscope and type. There are some interesting similarities and some intriguing relationships but no correlations. Perhaps the reason this question is raised so frequently is the way type is often reported to the client. Invariably, some set of personality portraits is given out with the report form. Because of the nature of type (with our overlapping preferences) we can often find something about ourselves in almost any of the sixteen types. Likewise, persons scanning the horoscopes in the newspaper can find things under several of the signs that seem to correspond with their lives. The similarities seem keen, but the limited research done does not justify the relationship.

Anecdotal evidence is rife. One of my senior consultants and dear friends was born on the same day and same year as I. We frequently kid each other in seminars as to who is older—we were born that close together. Our detailed astrological charts would look almost identical. We share many of the same concerns about developing people and both have a passion for creating organizational high performance. We are both "take charge Leos," if that technology excites you. However, we also have some significant differences:

- •I am a Christian; she is a Jew.
- •I am politically conservative; she is politically liberal.
- •I am straight; she is gay.
- •I am a Republican leaning toward Libertarian; she is a Democrat.
- •I am male; she is female.

• I am of German and British heritage; she is Russian.
• I am an INTJ; she is an ENFP.

It is just anecdotal data to be sure, but this is the case more times than not. Three studies of varying degrees of credibility over the years suggest there is no correlation between type and astrological sign.

QUESTION 9
Why do we have to pick between just two answers, (A) or (B)?

On 117 of the 126 questions on Form G of the MBTI®, one does have to choose between just (A) or (B). For eight of the questions there is also a (C) choice, and for one question there is also a (D) alternative. On form M, all the questions ask you to pick between just (A) and (B). While some types predictably find the A-B choices irritating, such a format merely reflects the dichotomous nature of Jung's theory. While all of us "E & I," "S & N," "T & F," and "J & P" at different times, we only do one at a time. In other words, before I begin to extravert, I have to stop introverting. I cannot "ambivert"! Consequently, at any given time I can only do one or the other. Since each question on the indicator deals with only one function or attitude pair, while I may (A) and (B) at different times, I can only do one at a time; hence, I have to choose. The preponderance of the times you pick (A) or (B) will show your preferences.

The indicator, therefore, differs from most other personality surveys that look at personality traits that can be expressed along a continuum. The MBTI® posits four pairs of neutral categories, none of which are good or bad, healthy or unhealthy, positive or negative. Furthermore, having one or more preference does not imply a deficit or lack of the opposite preferences.

Here's another way of looking at it. When an artilleryman learns gunnery, he or she learns how to hit a target with a round by first bracketing the target. He fires a round to the left (call that "A") and a round to the right (call that "B"). Once he sees where the rounds land, he narrows the bracket and fires two more rounds. He continues to narrow the bracket until the rounds fall directly on top of the target. The command then is "fire for effect," and the rounds land right on target. Something akin to that happens when completing the indicator. The client is asked to make 21 choices between "E" & "I," 26 choices between "S" & "N," 23 choices between "T" & "F," and 24 choices between "J" & "P." Once the client has indicated choices that many times (narrowed the bracket, if you will), the scorer can say "fire for effect." These are the four targets you have selected as your reported type.

The other aspect of the choices that often irritates people is the expectation that certain types (usually those with a "T" in their type formula) have that the choices be logically opposed. That, after all, has been the pattern established through years of test taking in school. The only problem is that the choices on the MBTI® are not necessarily *logical* opposites; instead, they are often *psychological* opposites. "Foundation" and "Spire" are not logical opposites in the way that the words "yes" and "no" or "white" and "black" are, but they are psychological opposites. The dichotomous nature of the choices, therefore, not only causes some interesting psychometric properties for the researcher (such as having bi-modal distributions for each of the four scales), but it also prompts some curious participant responses from folks who may wonder what "whacko" thought up these pairs.

QUESTION 10
I couldn't answer some of the questions. Will my results still be usable?

The short answer is, probably yes. It all depends on the number of omissions and how they are distributed. Unfortunately some consultants tell their clients that they have to answer *every* question on the indicator. That was never the authors' intent. The instructions for taking the MBTI® direct the client to answer as many questions as possible. If the client has no clear choice, however, he or she should leave the question unanswered.

The number of questions that can be left blank vary with the form being used. You can have up to thirty-five omissions for Form F, and up to twenty-five omissions for Form G as long as those omissions are roughly randomly distributed—i.e., not all omissions occur on one scale, for example. On form M, if you have four or more omissions on one of the attitude scales ("E-I" or "J-P") or five or more omissions on one of the function scales ("S-N" or "T-F"), you may not obtain valid results. I may ask you to re-look at the form and see if you can't answer a few more questions.

Over the years as I have scored hundreds of thousands of forms, when someone has left a large number of questions unanswered, over fifty, they have always fallen into one of three cases:

- •Reading challenged (They have never learned to read well or have a primary language different from the language in which the indicator is being administered),
- •They are fearful of the system (They do not know why the form is being administered or who gets the data), or
- •They are _NTP's. The INTP and the ENTP are two types most likely to leave multiple questions unanswered. They play devil's advocate, even with themselves, very well.

Yes, your answers will be usable.

QUESTION 11
Why do some Jungians reject the Judging-Perceiving distinction?

Isabel and Kathy developed Myers-Briggs Type Indicator®
specifically to make the theory of psychological types
described by C. G. Jung more accessible to the general
public. For many Jungians, having the Judging-Perceiving
attitude included on the form represents a violation of
Jungian theory. While the "J-P" difference was never
explicitly stated in Jung's writings, Katharine and Isabel
felt it was there implicitly. I, and others knowledgeable in
the field, agree with their judgment, but many "pure"
Jungians take umbrage at such liberties being taken with
the theory. "He didn't state it, so I don't believe it" tends
to be their mantra.

I like to help participants overcome any misgivings
regarding this distinction on the indicator by dividing
them into "J" and "P" groups and giving them a series of
assignments (Plan a meeting. / What to do with bonus
pay? / What should we do with the excess year-end
funds? / How should a teacher assign work for the day?
/ How should we use our tax refund? or some similar
exercise that will explore the difference between those
who want to schedule and control and those who prefer
to remain open to what occurs). Ironically, as I process the
results, the participants often see the "J"-"P" dichotomy
as one of the clearest to observe.

Jungians, as do other psychologists, also shudder anytime
someone other than a PhD. psychotherapist attempts to
use a personality survey to work with others. As a prac-
ticing engineer, English major, and ethicist, I take comfort
in the fact that neither Isabel nor Kathy was a psychologist, neither one had a graduate degree, and they devised

the indicator. I would rather send out an engineer, teacher, minister, German language major, or business manager who has spent one week studying with me to work with a client, than a psychotherapist with a terminal degree who might have studied a half dozen personality surveys sometime in an obscure graduate course last decade. Such is my heretical worldview.

QUESTION 12
Why do several questions seem to ask the same thing?

The issue is more than just "seeming." Many questions on the indicator do in fact attempt to elicit the same information. To some degree, there are only four questions on the indicator. We simply ask each question twenty to thirty times (See Question 9). By asking a series of seemingly inconsequential questions, the indicator attempts to elicit responses about eight preferences regarding human personality. For the most part, the more questions one asks about the same preferences, the higher the potential reliability of the results. The various shadings of the questions attempt to flesh out different possible understandings of what the questions mean, in an attempt to have those taking the indicator render the clearest possible results.

Some types (not unusually those with "N" and "T" preferences) will spot this feature of the indicator more quickly than others. Often, the temptation will be to try to be as consistent as possible in answering all the questions the same way, out of a concern that if they don't, such inconsistency might imply something negative or strange. Such conscious "gaming" ought to be discouraged. Simply try to respond honestly to each question.

QUESTION 13
Are intuitives more creative than sensors?

There is an unfortunately large number of consultants and creative thinking gurus who naively preach such a false gospel. No, intuitives are not more creative than sensors. The two are simply creative in different ways. The language I prefer to use to describe the difference comes from research I have done with another indicator: the KAI—Kirton-Adaption-Innovation Inventory (an indicator designed by the Brit, M. J. Kirton). For six years while I was the Director of Personal Development at the AFSC, National Defense University, I was able to research correlations between KAI results and MBTI® results for about 6,000 commissioned officers from all U. S. military services, senior civilians from all federal agencies, and senior officers from several other countries. The KAI, which measures one's style of creativity, posits the difference between generative creativity (an innovative style) and adaptive creativity. Not only because there are correlations between the two but also because the terms so aptly describe the process, I use the term *Generative* to describe the intuitive's style of creativity and the term *Adaptive* to describe the sensor's style. Routinely, on the KAI scale, "N's" and "P's" tend to be to the right of center and "S's" and "J's" tend to fall to the left of center.

Adaptive ——————————|—————————— Generative

An intuitive, in being creative, is likely to scrap the entirety of what is currently being done. Whatever the current paradigm, it is up for grabs in the intuitive's search for a more creative way. If that paradigm is a system, a procedure, a set of rules, a tradition, or a customary way of doing things in an organization, then it should be clear why the intuitive is oftentimes seen as a little disruptive to the status quo. Sensors will see the intuitive as not as "safe" as the more "stable" sensor who works within the system, or the current paradigm, to accomplish change. By contrast, in being more comfortable with what is and what has been, the sensor adapts his or her creativity to the existing framework and, therefore, can appear to be the better team player—more supportive of the organization. On the other hand, the intuitive sees the sensors as slow and uncreative in their thinking. But of course there is a tradeoff between the two styles.

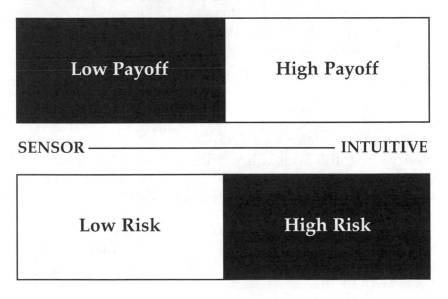

Low Payoff	High Payoff

SENSOR ———————————————— **INTUITIVE**

Low Risk	High Risk

Sensors' preferences can make them highly successful and effective working within existing organizational systems. They tend to capitalize on existing definitions and likely solutions. They are able to stretch the "givens" in new and creative ways. They focus on producing change using existing methods for improvement. But there is both good news and bad news about their style. The good news is that they are frequently successful in their efforts at change; the bad news is that the increment of success each time is likely to be relatively low.

Intuitives perceive quite differently! They tend to redefine the entire problem. They are often more concerned with doing something differently than with doing an established, standardized procedure better. Their solutions are less expected and in some cases less accepted. More innovative than adaptive, intuitives tend to go outside the established systems and methods for solutions. The good news is that when they are successful, the payoff can be very high. The bad news is that they tend to be successful at a much lower frequency than are the sensors. These differences in styles of creativity between sensors and intuitives, if not understood in terms of preferred style, can create havoc and interpersonal confusion within any organization.

One activity I use to underscore the differences between how "S's" and "N's" exercise their different forms of creativity I adapted from James Adams' book, *Conceptual Blockbusting*. I have sensors and intuitives each respond to the following situation in groups. I tell them they are locked in a room with four concrete walls, concrete ceiling and concrete floor. The ceiling is too high to reach in any way, and in the ceiling there is a bright light that illuminates the entire room. They can take nothing into the room with them.

Embedded in the floor is a standard lead pipe. It extends four inches out of the floor. The interior diameter of the pipe is 1.5 inches. Inside the pipe, resting on the concrete four inches inside the pipe, is a ping pong ball. There is a total clearance between the interior sides of the pipe and the ping pong ball of .04 inches. Your task is to get the ping pong ball out of the pipe without damaging the ping pong ball, the pipe, or the connection between the pipe and the concrete. You have, to assist you and your team,

- a pipe wrench
- a box of Wheaties
- a standard metal rasp file
- a wood chisel (half inch tip)
- a wooden handle, claw hammer
- 100 feet of clothes line
- one wire coat hanger
- a 100 watt light bulb

and nothing else. I give the two groups fifteen minutes to develop their suggestions. Whenever I give classes this exercise to think about, the intuitives dream up more solutions than the sensors—usually ten to twelve. However, when I actually put these two groups in a room with a real pipe, embedded in real concrete and real equipment, and challenge them to solve the problem, the sensors always solve the problem in more ways than do the intuitives. The intuitives "generate" more solutions in the abstract, but when the sensors are immersed in the facticity of things, they "adapt" to more solutions. Which group sounds more creative to you?

Once managers become skilled in the recognition of these differences in individuals or organizations, they can be much more effective in accomplishing organizational objectives. Where the sensor's and intuitive's styles complement one another, we have a richer base for creativity. The sensor provides a safe base for the intuitive's riskier operations, and the intuitive provides the dynamics to bring about periodic radical change, without which institutions tend to ossify.

True creativity may be the ability to respond to new situations effectively ("N") as well as apply learnings from

71

one's past experiences ("S"). *Neither sensors nor intuitives are more creative than the other.*

QUESTION 14
What do very high scores or very low scores indicate about a person? Which is better?

The short answer is that neither high nor low scores are necessarily good or bad. Unlike basketball, the high score does not win, and unlike golf, the low score does not win. There are, however, tradeoffs with each. First of all, the words "high" and "low" are red flags to many people. We are a numbers oriented culture. From the earliest grades we learn that high IQ is good and low IQ means trouble. We unfortunately associate "high" with good and "low" with bad. The association probably stems back to a concern with grades in school. A score of 98 on a math test is cause for celebration and maybe a stop at the Dairy Queen on the way home from school, but a 55 on the same test means a stern meeting with Dad when he comes home from work at 6:00 pm. Regretfully, the report forms used by most people to communicate preference strengths to clients also perpetuate this unconscious association, as does the publisher's newest reporting mechanism for form M.

In an effort to reflect faithfully the dichotomous nature of the theory and the scores on all forms up to and including form G, they are routinely sketched on a horizontal continuum with zero in the middle and the extremes to the left and the right. The scores for "E," "S," "T," & "J" are reported to the left of center, and the scores for "I," "N," "F," & "P" are reported to the right of center. Unfortunately we also learned in school that negative numbers are to the left and positive numbers are to the right. While this is a subtle influence to be sure, it may, nevertheless, be at work in a client's mind.

Rather than use the words "high" and "low" to describe preference strengths, I prefer the terms from *The Manual: Slight, Moderate, Clear,* and *Very Clear.* These terms connote less regarding relative desirability than do "high" or "low," or "strong" or "weak." When I report data out to a client, I use a circular mandala to sketch the relative clarity of preferences for those who are more visual than auditory. Not only does this form eliminate the up—down, left—right, good—bad relationships among the preferences and numbers, but the mandala is more Jungian.

There are both good points and bad points associated with *very clear* preferences (41 or higher; 31 for "F"). What is known is *only* that the individual has a definite preference for that function or attitude. It may well be that the individual also has more ability with that preference because it is used more—much like a muscle that gets stronger by frequent exercise—but we do not know that. What we know is that persons with very clear preferences *know* their preferences, and by extrapolation, perhaps they know themselves better. The bad news is that when called upon to use the opposite preference, a person with such clarity of preferences often finds it more difficult to do the opposite.

The person with *slight* preferences (1-9) faces a somewhat different set of circumstances. On the plus side of the ledger, such a person may have greater ease in moving from one end of the spectrum to the other; perhaps that person can do both with some ease, even though he or she still has a preference. The bad news is that such persons may themselves not know when they will do one or the other. Such a dilemma can cause confusion for the persons themselves and may well send mixed signals to others on the job.

Let's say a colleague has a "J" preference strength of 3 on form G. On Monday, someone sees her and asks for a decision. "Do it," she says. "It sounds like a feasible course of action." She acts "J" and makes a decision, as we expect her to do. On Tuesday, you present her with three courses of action on an upcoming customer service problem. She says, "Implement number two." Again, she decides true to type, given her "J." On Wednesday, I come in with a report I have been working on. It needs her approval before the report can go forward to the CFO. "Oh," she says, "Let's hold off on sending this until we gather some more data on the soil samples at the Monroe plant." That comment—just born from her desire to play "P" for the day—runs the risk of telling me that I have blundered, I've missed the boat on the report, I failed to get the pertinent data. I've screwed up.

While neither very clear nor slight preferences are necessarily good or bad, it is apparent from Jung's writings that he thought that persons ought to be clear about their preferences. A person with a slight strength can *know* his or her preference, and just understand that it is not very demonstrative. But Jung would warn that a person with slight preferences runs the risk of never truly developing them, and that would keep all preferences relatively underdeveloped—what he referred to as a "primitive mentality."

The important point to underscore, however, with anyone who has taken the indicator is that *"strength does not imply excellence."* The fact that I score I-57, N-51, T-29, and J-45, does not mean that I necessarily do any of them well; Nor does it suggest, as some who use the TDI will tell you, that I lack balance or worse. Those kinds of judgments just are not warranted. All high scores indicate is that I have clear or very clear preferences throughout. Preference strengths do not measure maturity, capability, intelligence, skill, ability, or development—simply preference. While it is just an analogy, type preference is similar to right-handedness or left-handedness. We all have a preference, and we all can exercise the opposite behavior if we have to, but when we do, some one might say, he or she doesn't seem like himself or herself today; it might just feel a little awkward.

QUESTION 15
What does Balance mean
in Type Theory?

There is a crucial distinction to be made between balance between preferences and balance as understood in Jungian theory. Balance as implied in this question would suggest relative equality of "E & I," "S & N," "T & F," or "J & P." In other words, what is being implied is balance horizontally along the four dichotomous scales. *Balance* in type theory, however, is something altogether different.

	B	
Extraversion———	A	———Introversion
Sensing———	L	———Intuition
Thinking———	A	———Feeling
Judging———	N	———Perceiving
	C	
	E	

Balance in type theory is vertical, not horizontal. *Balance*, then would be balance between the Perceiving Function ("S" or "N") and the Judging Function ("T" or "F"). Because, by definition, one of these two functions is dominant in a person's type and the other is auxiliary, *Balance* could also be defined as having a dominant function working together as a team with the auxiliary. And lastly, since by definition, if the dominant is expressed in an extraverted attitude, the auxiliary is introverted, or if the dominant is expressed in an introverted attitude, the auxiliary is extraverted, *Balance* also implies a balance between the outer world and the inner world (See Question 37).

To recap, *Balance* is vertical between the Perceiving and the Judging functions not horizontal along lines. Indeed, if a person has several or all of his or her preferences within the "slight" category (balanced horizontally like a teeter-totter on a fulcrum), the data may be important, but it reveals nothing at all about *Balance* (see Question 14).

It is very important that this concept be understood. Some very well-known trainers muddy the waters in regard to this concept. By using the Jungian language, they confuse the issue, and a person can infer that they recommend more or less equal amounts of each of the eight preferences in a successful leader. That was never Jung's intention. So what begins as a good notion—using the appropriate preference at the appropriate time—becomes flawed because of their too casual use of the word "balance." Proper use of language and definition of terms is critical when dealing with type theory (See Question 24).

QUESTION 16
Can the MBTI® be used for psychologically disturbed people?

The indicator has a wellness framework. This is one of the reasons why I choose to use the MBTI® almost exclusively in my company. Other forms like the FIRO-B, DISC, LIFO, MMPI, and Enneagram are capable of giving us interesting insights; however, the wellness orientation of the MBTI® sets it apart from the lot.

The close relationship between Carl Gustav Jung and his

mentor, Sigmund Freud, hit the rocks over their disagreement around the nature of "disease." For Carl Jung, one of whose several earned academic degrees was in medicine, the word disease actually meant "dis.......ease," not at ease. In other words, disease happens, according to Jung, when human beings, for whatever reason, no longer feel capable of bringing their bodies, their minds, and their spirits together in some holistic way. Let's use the "m" word. Disease happens in marriages when a partner believes, for whatever reason, that she or he can no longer bring to that relationship their body, their mind, or their spirit with a sense of authenticity. In marriages, we call that disease divorce, separation, or in California, "walking our separate paths." In businesses, we call it downsizing, rightsizing, or strike.

In our business, we want to find a way to eliminate disease. Our conviction is that you can do just that when leaders at every level of the organization make a concerted effort to nurture a culture where every individual is not only allowed but encouraged to bring to work each day 100 % of their own uniqueness and diversity in terms of body, mind, and spirit. When that happens, things change dramatically.

The normative work done to establish the form's reliability, validity, and other psychometric properties was, as best we know, on non-psychiatric audiences. Thus, any use of the indicator with psychologically disturbed persons should be done with the understanding that the results may not be meaningful. Some individuals have done work with the indicator on persons with multiple personalities and others outside the norm. While current thinking may not include such individuals in the dysfunctional category, I do. Such use was not the intention of the indicator. There is, therefore, no reason to assume that the results are meaningful.

QUESTION 17
Do "TJ's" make the best top-level managers?

Frequently, the reluctance to take the Myers-Briggs Type Indicator® stems from the fear that some of the partici-pants are going to be told that, based on their results, they just won't make it to the top. The good news is that the indicator doesn't provide those kinds of answers. No type is good; no type is bad. No type is destined to make it to the top; no type is predisposed to fail. My personal research and testing demonstrates that there are CEO's, presidents, and board chairs of the world's largest corpo-rations in each of the sixteen squares of the type table (See Question 62). I have also seen the results of senior mili-tary officers in the five United States Services that indicate they also select each of the sixteen types, just some with greater frequency than others. There is no ideal type!

But it is one thing to say who makes the best senior man-agers and another to say which types tend to predomi-nate the upper echelons of leadership. While each of the types has shown itself capable of making it to the top, cer-tain types do tend to predominate. The four corners of the type table (ISTJ, INTJ, ESTJ, and ENTJ) are found in great abundance at the top echelons of leadership. Some of the firms I have worked with have in excess of 90 % of their top three tiers of management in just those four descrip-tions. Routinely, the percentage is over 62 %. The data would suggest that whatever the system, be it govern-ment, church, university, public school administration, the corporate world, or virtually any other, while all types are found in the trenches doing the actual work, at least 62 % of the top levels of management are found in the four cor-ners of the type table: the "TJ's" that prompted the ques-tion. In manufacturing companies, this figure routinely exceeds 65%.

Let's look at three levels of organizational leadership to

TABLE 1

Chief Executive Officers: n = 185
Executive Vice Presidents/Senior Vice Presidents: n = 55,590
Middle Managers and Supervisors: n=1,565,000

	CEO	EVP/SVP	MM/S
ISTJ	2.8	29.8	23.9
ISFJ	0	1.7	4.7
INFJ	0	1.0	1.5
INTJ	26.0	9.8	7.2
ISTP	8.6	4.3	4.1
ISFP	0	1.1	1.5
INFP	2.8	1.5	2.1
INTP	11.4	5.6	4.9
ESTP	2.8	3.4	3.9
ESFP	2.8	.8	1.1
ENFP	8.6	2.4	2.7
ENTP	2.8	7.2	7.3
ESTJ	5.7	17.6	18.8
ESFJ	0	1.5	2.8
ENFJ	5.7	1.1	1.6
ENTJ	20.0	11.2	11.9
TJ's	54.5 %	68.4 %	61.8 %

see who tends to be where. The three groups expressed in Table 1 are CEO's, Executive Vice Presidents, and Middle Managers. The data comes from our current client base of approximately 166 Fortune 500 Companies, all five United States Military Services, all United States Federal

Government agencies, entrepreneurial companies, several privately-owned companies and family-run businesses, and some start-up ventures in thirty-six countries.

The data is broken down by the percent of the respective sample found in each type category. Furthermore, unlike most of the data published in the *Journal of Psychological Type* or presented at conferences, our data all reflects participant-validated types. As this book goes to print, the data reflects the sample sizes shown in Table 1.

Does the frequency of the "TJ's" in Table 1 mean that these individuals make the best top-level managers? No. What it means is that those who have the preference to make analytic, impersonal, objective, logical decisions based on the cause-and-effect relationship between the data ("T's") and the preference to order, structure, schedule, and otherwise arrive at closure based on their analysis ("J's"), have tended to rise to the top of the corporate ladder, or to have "stuck it out" better than have most other types. These four types are those who are sometimes called the "tough-minded executives" for whom the bottom line is getting the products out the door. But, to reiterate, this fact does not mean that these individuals are the best. Empirically, that is just who we find there in the largest numbers.

There are some trainers who, almost in a normative way, suggest that "TJ's" belong in such positions and that they are more effective in running organizations. Furthermore, they suggest that the current state of affairs, where the "TJ's" are in charge, will continue into the foreseeable future. That proposition is just an opinion, however, and an unwarranted one. To make such a normative claim flies in the face of diversity and disadvantages at least twelve of the types who may make as equally fine organizational leaders.

In the last several years, more and more "N's," "F's," and "P's" have been moving into the upper ranks of corporations and government organizations. For example, four of the last five CEO's who have assumed the helm of Fortune 500 companies, have been _NFP's. In a business environment where vision, values, and an ability to grow people are increasingly praised, these preferences seem fitting. For the moment, however, let no one be misled, *the "TJ's" are in charge!*

QUESTION 18
How effective can the MBTI® be in reflecting the Types of individuals from different cultures or nationalities?

It depends on what you mean by the MBTI®. If the question is probing whether or not non-native English speakers who are, however, fluent in English, report that the indicator has adequately reflected their preferences, the validated data is sparse. Most information regarding this issue is anecdotal and hinges on whether, after receiving a competent presentation on the theory, preferences, and results and reading one of the type portraits on the market, the individual thinks the portrait sounds on target.

In the last thirteen years, our company has administered the American English version of Forms F and G to about 171,400 non-native "American English" speakers from the following countries: Argentina, Australia, Austria, Bahamas, Belgium, Brazil, Cambodia, Canada, Chile, China, Cuba, The Dominican Republic, England, Egypt, Fiji, Finland, France, Germany, Haiti, Hungary, India, Indonesia, Iran, Iraq, Israel, Italy, Jamaica, Jordan, Kenya, Korea, Luxembourg, Malaysia, Mexico, The Netherlands, New Zealand, Nigeria, Norway, Pakistan, The Philippines, Puerto Rico, Romania, Russia, Saudi Arabia, Singapore, Spain, The Sudan, Sweden, Taiwan, Thailand, Turkey, Vietnam, and Zimbabwe. The percentage of those individuals (all highly educated and fluent in English)

81

who agreed with their reported type was over 70 %. This percentage is higher than the percent of presumed English speakers who agreed with their reported types in the 1985 *Manual*.

The more important question may be which version of the MBTI® has a non-native English speaker taken? Jung's theory clearly is not intended just for North Americans. Currently, the indicator is available in several languages (49 at this printing). The only question yet to be resolved is how well the indicator has been prepared for the various countries where it is in use. One cannot *just translate* the English version. Indeed, one cannot even just *transliterate* it. What is vital is that the indicator be normed for the culture for which it is intended. It must be *transculturated*. I don't think you'll find that word in any dictionary. It was born out of our own work with European and African audiences.

Some non-English language versions are trustworthy and some are not. Knowing firsthand the quality of translation and normative procedures that have gone into the German version, for example, I am confident it will be reviewed as one of the best available. I have also used the French, Spanish, and Italian versions with confidence for several years. I have used the Portuguese research version in Brazil for several years with great success, and the Italian version always gets good reviews as well. The Chinese version, on the other hand, is not viewed as very trustworthy by our colleagues working in Mainland China or in Taiwan. Some other versions need to be used even more cautiously. *Buena suerte!* (When in doubt, trust the client not the form.)

Interest in cross-cultural applications of the MBTI® is growing dramatically. There is now an International Council and an APT Cross-Cultural Committee.

Fortunately, international interest in type has grown immensely in the last decade. But, quite frankly, I am personally disturbed by the glib approach we in the type community take to try to understand type around the world. I find many of the workshops at type conferences puerile at best because of the conclusions presenters try to draw based on extremely limited samples from several countries. The articles published in *The Journal of Psychological Type* and the "Bulletin of Psychological Type" also lead readers to conclude erroneously about type distributions around the world, based on limited sample sizes.

Clearly, people are different around the world. Those of you who travel widely are aware of hundreds of cultural issues that we face as we travel, let alone train, negotiate, communicate, or try to build relationships. A hand gesture that is acceptable in the United States may well get your tires slashed in Brazil. Crossing one's legs when a person sits may be fine in Chicago but highly offensive in Vietnam or Djibouti. Chewing gum in New Jersey may be fine, but the same activity in Singapore may well get you publicly caned. People are truly different, and we can revel in that diversity as we travel.

However, type around the world seems to be relatively consistent. Indeed, in all of the twenty-nine countries where we routinely work, the general culture is more extraverted than introverted, more sensing than intuitive, more thinking than feeling, and more judging than perceiving. We are an ESTJ world. That data includes six Asian countries where North Americans routinely see the native population as introverted. It is just that what looks like introverted behavior through western eyes is, in the context of their own culture, extraverted. Properly understanding "transculturation" is critical to our more professional understanding of type differences

83

and similarities.

On the other hand, while the general population data worldwide is relatively consistent, the types of those who rise to the top in each culture or country are quite different. Different cultures value different leadership styles; therefore, the types that rise to the top in different countries vary greatly. In the United States, for example, while the general population is split approximately 50 %-50 % on the Thinking-Feeling function, the military, as a whole, is 92 % "T," male and female combined. In the private sector, the top three tiers of leadership is 93 % T.

When we travel to Europe, similar results apply. Now, I do not mean to sound monolithic. I would be the first to remind us of the vast diversity within the various countries we roughly refer to as Europe, but let's take northern Europe (Germany, France, Luxembourg, Belgium, The Netherlands, Austria, Norway, and Sweden). The top three tiers of leadership of multinational companies in northern Europe—the further south and east we go, the more this mediates—are 97 % "T." While this figure is relatively the same as North America, as we travel east the data changes dramatically.

Join me in Japan. Now, the data in Thailand, The Philippines, Vietnam, China, Taiwan, Korea, and Indonesia are roughly the same (within about ten percentage points—Singapore is an anomaly), but since so much economic news is directed at Japan, let's focus there. The general population is roughly 50 % "T" and 50 % "F" (with the usual male-female bias expected), but the top three tiers of leadership in Japan report 72 % "F." The Japanese Diet—roughly equivalent to the United States Congress—is 86 % "F."

My experience in Japan is that if you want to do business

in Japan, you have to be prepared to "F" around for a while. No effing, no business. You have to "F" at Karaoke, "F" on the golf course, "F" at supper, "F" at the baths, "F" everywhere. Major effing is required! That is most likely why the ESFJ, the ENFP, and the ESFP are the most successful sales types in the Asian Rim. These types know very well that you have to build the relationship first, sometimes even before you discuss the technical capabilities of the products being sold. The relationship is primary!

It is no wonder that the typical North American approach to working in Japan yields less than satisfactory results. Too often North American companies expect to send over three or four vice presidents and the chief counsel to negotiate a deal for four or five days. At the end of the negotiations, we expect an agreement to be signed obligating each of the parties to certain actions in the future. We sign on the dotted line, shake hands, and the deal becomes law. Where is the "F" in that?

When my wife was a new chemical engineer, fresh out of the University of Wisconsin, Madison, she would travel frequently with the president of a large German chemical corporation as he was involved in high-level negotiations in Japan. She would have a chance to sit in the back of the room and watch and learn. On one occasion, Mr. Yakasawa, the president of a Japanese company, brought his female secretary in to sit next to her so she would not be the only female in the conference room. That is Japanese graciousness at its best—it is also "F."

Three years ago, my wife had a chance to return to the same conference room, this time representing a different company. She arrived this time to acquire the Japanese company. As luck would have it, Mr. Yakasawa was still there as the Chairman of the Board. I remember watching as she walked up to him and bowed and politely asked, "Yakasawa-san, may I sit at your table today?" "Indeed, you may," he responded politely. "It will probably be your table tomorrow." After effing around for several days, Mr. Yakasawa said, "Cheryl, I find all this very interesting. You and I have now agreed to the major elements of the acquisition. You now have to return to the United States and secure final approval from your Chairman. I have to receive final approval from my employees." That difference, folks, is "F."

During the year 2001, we watched a series of events unfold between the United Staes and Asia that took the Thinking-Feeling distinction to the heart of foreign policy. On one occasion, an American fast attack submarine—*The USS Greenville*—did an immediate action drill and blew ballast about 100 feet and surfaced, killing nine Japanese students and crew as it squashed a fishing boat used for educational purposes. For the first time in history, a sitting American Secretary of State apologized immediately to a foreign government for a military action. He did so because Colin Powell, an "F," understands very well the Japanese need for relationship.

In the weeks following the Secretary's apology, the skipper of the submarine, an Annapolis graduate, also apologized—over the advice of counsel—and, in a very emotional press conference, asked to meet with the families of the victims so he could apologize to them as well. The navy commander was excoriated in the *Navy Times* for weeks until he finally resigned from active service. He had done the moral thing and paid the price for his values, even as the Japanese dropped several of the lawsuits they had filed against the United States. That's "F"!

Think also about the controversy in the year 2001 over the "apology" the United States made to the Chinese when an American "spy" plane was attacked and forced down by the Chinese Air Force. For weeks, the press tried to parse what an apology was or was not, what it meant in Chinese or one of the multiple translations we received of it. Congress persons with their usual bloated hubris huffed and puffed from both sides of the aisle telling the world why what the United States did was wrong.

What was the result? The United States got all crewmembers back unharmed in just a few days, and the Lockheed Martin manufactured aircraft was sent home as well. And China managed to save face by requiring that the plane be sent back in crates after they had gone over it. At the time, the majority of the military officers who run China were "T's" (some had been through parts of the United States War College system and had taken the MBTI®), and the majority of the civilians who currently pretend to be in charge of China are "F's." The apology had to meet both sets of needs. An apology for a "T" is not an apology to an "F." It is often just an excuse.

QUESTION 19
What are word pairs, and why do some people report this data to the client?

Some consultants, Executive Strategies International among them, report to the client both overall preference strengths and word pair strengths if the word pairs point to a different preference from the overall. Let me explain. There are at least six separate groupings of data available to be read when a person takes form F or G of the MBTI®.

Overall Scale
Phrase Questions
Word Pairs
X Split-Half Score
Y Split-Half Score
Unscored questions

Of these, the ones we report to the client are the *Overall Scale* and the *Word Pairs.* The overall scale is simply the sum of the phrase questions (those that give a context to the question) and the word pairs (those that ask the client to pick a single, non-contextual word), or the sum of the X and Y split-half scores. Any one of the first five scales listed is capable of rendering type independently from the rest. The unscored questions are simply those questions that are not recorded on the scoring keys but can be studied for other issues.

The word pairs did not appear on the indicator until Form F (166 questions). They were added because the author found that some types would read the phrase questions and instead of responding generally to their choices, would reflect back on the last time they found themselves in that situation and vote more or less specifically (The last time I did that I ...). Since that was not the intent of the question, the author tried to find another method of eliciting the same data. The word pairs, stripped of a context, provide that naked chance for preference. Ironically, the data indicated they were more valid than the phrase questions, but they lacked "face validity." In short, respondents didn't think they were valid. So, most of the phrase questions remain.

The reason we report the word pairs is that for some people they may provide some insights not available in just the overall score. If on the word pairs an individual reports preferences that differ from the overall score, we report that difference to the client. It is additional information that may help the client better ascertain true type or understand why there may be perceived behavioral differences at different times. There are at least three hypotheses as to what these word pairs may mean. Please hear, these are just "hypotheses." There may be more. Word pairs may give a clearer indication of how a person comes across to others spontaneously. They may also help clients see differences between their "work self" and their "at home self," or between how they see themselves and how they wish they could be.

On form G, we find about 11 % of those completing the form have at least one difference between overall preferences and word pair preferences. A current study our firm is running indicates that for those who have made it to the top echelons of organizations, the percentage of those with differences between the type reported in the word pairs and the type reported in the overall scores is less than 3 %. Thus, the preliminary data suggests that knowing our preferences clearly may assist in helping us achieve more senior positions within executive ranks.

On form M, there are no unscored or research questions. They have been removed for brevity. Also, the researchers who developed form M report no differences in the psychometric properties of word pairs and phrases on Form M. They suggest there is no need to report word pairs separately on that form. Until form M data becomes significant, I'll withhold judgment on the validity of their claims.

QUESTION 20
My preference for Introversion has gotten stronger the older I have become.
Is that unusual?

No, not at all. There has not been much research done to explore the relationship between aging and type. In fact it is one of the real gaps in scholarship that must be corrected as we age as a country. About all we know is that—all things being equal—our preferences tend to become clearer as we age. The one preference where we notice significant shifts is in introversion. As we age, we seem to become more comfortable with our introversion. Don't forget, introverts live in an extraverted conspiracy. The population seems to be about 70 % extraverted. (This has been an accepted figure in the type community for decades. The new *Manual* may call this percentage into question, but their sample is pathetically small and unimpressive). Thus, there is great pressure to develop extraverted skills. As we mature, we seem to become more comfortable acting on our preferences–particularly, it seems, if one of them is introversion. When this happens, it is often exciting to watch someone finally give himself or herself permission to be themselves: just what Jung intended to happen. We sometimes call this behavior eccentricity; Jung saw it as growth.

QUESTION 21
Are there any discernible racial differences or patterns reflected in our types?

This is a good question, and unfortunately we have precious little data upon which to draw. We face that dilemma for a number of reasons. Foremost is that for years, nowhere on the demographic portion of the answer sheet was there a place for clients to report their race; hence, the data on types has not been kept by race, and any attempt to do so may invoke concerns as to why the question is being asked. Furthermore, even though the MBTI® is reaching more and more people from diverse socio-economic and educational groupings, the normative data gathered thus far is still based predominantly on white, middle class, high school- and college-educated audiences. For this reason, any use of population percentages of the various types has to be done circumspectly. Our company's work in Africa and among other persons of color in this country and elsewhere is beginning to add legitimacy to the type database, but progress has been slow.

Even with the substantial recent work done by

researchers in preparation for form M, trying to provide a new national adult sample for standardization, the process was flawed racially. The exact breakdowns of the various groups surveyed can be found in the third edition of *The Manual* (pp. 156-7), but suffice it to say that white women were over-represented and black men were under-represented in the sample. For that reason, the small size of the samples used, and many other reasons, I tend to dismiss population norms cited by the publisher. I will stick with our company's sample that numbers in the millions.

But the question of the relationship between race and type is still broader. My experience is that those of any non-majority grouping face, perhaps more than most, the potential problem of "falsification of type" (See Question 23). To what extent do I allow environmental factors to inhibit my reporting my true preferences? Often it is the non-majority members of any organization who hear the echoes of "shape up or ship out." To a certain extent, "minorities" (this might be a person with a Boston accent in Charlotte, North Carolina, a Jew in the Vatican, or a WASP like me in Harlem) both consciously and unconsciously are drawn to report the behaviors (and perhaps the types) of the majority. Upon personal interview, these individuals often admit to substantial differences between reported type and true type.

QUESTION 22
Some consultants use letter combinations of "ST," "SF," "NF," & "NT." Others use "SJ" & "SP" in lieu of "ST" & "SF." What is the difference?

The difference is between those who hold to a stricter *FUNCTION THEORY* approach to type and those who marry type theory with David Keirsey's observations about *TEMPERAMENT* (see *Please Understand Me*).

Often the difference in practice has been prompted by where the person was trained. Some Qualifying Workshops stress function pairs and emphasize the Jungian nature of type; others introduce temperament as a viable model for understanding human behavior.

Those who prefer function theory link one of the Perceiving functions (Sensing or Intuition) with one of the Judging functions (Thinking or Feeling): "SF," "ST," "NF," and "NT." Those persons who prefer Temperament theory mix one of the Perceiving functions (Sensing), with one of the attitudes that indicate our orientation to the outer world (Judging or Perceiving), "SJ" and "SP," and one of the Perceiving functions (Intuition) with the two Judging functions (Thinking or Feeling), "NF" and "NT." It is to many merely a matter of preference—which pairings give the examples of overt behavior in the clearest way.

I personally find both models useful and take different approaches depending on the typological and career makeup of the group I am addressing, always aware that I am on sounder theoretical underpinnings if I use function pairs rather than temperament. I must confess, however, that in business settings I see clearer differences using temperament groupings than function pairs.

If I am working with groups of teachers, clergy, or educators, I often break the groups up into function pairs and ask them to perform certain tasks in order to highlight behavioral differences among the groups. If I am working with business audiences or military groups, I use temperament groupings because they routinely show clearer behavioral outcomes and can help individuals sort out true type from reported type.

QUESTION 23
What is meant by "falsification of type?"

"Falsification" of type can occur when individuals have allowed environmental issues—the overwhelming facticity of what developmental psychologists call "nurture"—to mask, interfere with, overwhelm, or otherwise get in the way of their reporting their genuine preferences. It may be some kind of pressure they feel to report themselves a certain way. What we are really talking about, although we shy away from using such language in MBTI® circles, is faking our responses. It is a well-studied phenomenon in psychometric circles that looks at the tendency of an individual to produce responses that he or she knows are necessary to fit in. Rather than be truthful, we sometimes adopt a "popular" stance instead. In more Jungian terms, one of our masks has taken over and become the person.

A serious issue, falsification of type may interfere with a person's natural type development and hinder true individuation (see Question 24). Jung, himself, was particularly sensitive to this issue, and one of the driving forces in his psychology was the concern he felt that too often people were discouraged or prevented from becoming the persons they were truly meant to be.

Borrowing from Schopenhauer, Jung believed that every living thing had a unique core of what it was uniquely intended to be. Inside of an oak tree, for example, is something that says, "grow up and become an oak tree." It is not to the acorn's advantage to aspire to produce a weeping willow. It won't happen. Similarly, inside of every human being is something that tells us what we are uniquely intended to be—call that our true type—if we will pay attention to it. Unfortunately, the system—sometimes that system is called the family, sometimes it is the church or synagogue or mosque, sometimes it is the

93

school, and sometimes it is a job—tells us to shape up or ship out. Human beings naturally try to seek pleasure and avoid pain, and so we falsify our type to fit in. Sometimes that falsification is conscious and purposeful, and sometimes it is unconscious.

Our source of true personal power and influence stems from our ability to exercise our true type. I had the chance to offer the MBTI® to one rather well-known military client on four occasions. We'll call him Andy. Andy's name was in the news many years ago when a C-130 blew up in the Iranian Desert outside of Teheran. On the first three times Andy took the indicator, he reported ISTJ. As many of you know, this is the "military" type. The type accounts for about 6 % of the world's population but 34 % of everybody in uniform around the world reports ISTJ. The military is over one third one type and one type only. The ISTJ type comprises about 60 % of the FBI, 70 % of all the graduates of Navy's Top Gun School, and 29.5 % of all executive vice presidents and above of multinational companies. It is, in short, a highly responsible type. It is the backbone of every large and complex organization. Their word is their bond! So, Andy fit the mold for twenty-six years. He reported ISTJ as an army major, army colonel, and army brigadier general (one star).

The last time Andy took the indicator, he reported INTP. This time he was a lieutenant general (three stars). These two types are remarkably different. Talk to an ISTJ and it is like standing on granite. Talk to an INTP and it is like standing on shifting tectonic plates; they can change universes mid-sentence. I remember asking, "So, Andy, three times ISTJ and one time INTP, what are you going to be when you grow up?" Or, as I usually phrase it when I am coaching a senior executive, "What is your true type?" Andy looked at me and said, "Bill, I think you know my true type as well as I do." I said, "Andy, I think I have

seen your true type for twenty-six years." "You're right,"
he admitted. "I'm an INTP and always have been. But
you know what, Bill? For twenty-six years I knew how to
get ahead; for twenty-six years I knew what sold. I could
out-ISTJ any ISTJ I worked with; I was darn good at it!
But in my case, it took two divorces, a heart attack, and
the suicide of my eight-year-old son to finally realize I
didn't always have to be right ['J'], and I didn't always
need to have all the facts ['S']." That is a little bit of
growth.

I want people to figure out, before they reach 56 years of
age and find themselves in their last job, what their true
type is. Our true type is the true source of all true power
and authority we have. In the very dangerous world in
which we live today, businesses, relationships, political
systems, and military units need individuals coming to
work with their true types each day (See Question 2).

QUESTION 24
What is "individuation" and how does it differ from or relate to "good type development"?

With this question, we have have moved clearly into
advanced material. The terms "balance" (see Question
15), "good type development," and "individuation" are
all intertwined. It is hard to discuss one without the other.
Individuation is the goal of Jungian psychology—the
apex of good type development—which all of us should
strive for but which very few of us reach. It is, in short,
the "lifelong process of becoming the complete human
beings we were born to be." To use Robert A. Johnson's
metaphor, it is the "actualizing of the blueprint" (*Inner
Work*, p. 11). Let me explain.

On one consulting assignment in Europe, I had occasion
to meet two German colleagues in Köln (Cologne). We
agreed to meet on the steps of the main entrance to the

95

Dom—one of the world's greatest cathedrals and architec-
tural wonders. It is an immense gothic cathedral that
dwarfs all around it and dominates the horizon of the city
for miles. As one gets closer, he or she becomes aware
that during the construction, over hundreds of years, the
style of architecture changed: spires were added, flying
buttresses were expanded, great stained glass windows
were commissioned and included, until what transpired
was an awesome tribute to humankind's efforts to capture, in one building, what the theologian St. Augustine
would have called the City of Man meeting the City of
God. It is as though, despite the hundreds of changes
made over the centuries, that a grand blueprint of what a
cathedral should look like had been there all along and
had finally taken form. And notice, it was not a static
form. There had been a basic blueprint (you might call
that "nature"), but that basic form had been modified
through the years (you might call that "nurture")(see
Question 1).

Well, it is just a metaphor, but a notion not too dissimilar
was what Jung had in mind for individuation. He seems
to have gotten the concept from Schopenhauer, who
talked about the *principium individuationis*, that seed
within each living thing that determines what it was
uniquely designed to be. There is, for example, something inside the tulip that says grow and become a tulip,
not a tiger lily. Likewise, in each of us there is someone
who we are meant to become. The tragedy from Jung's
perspective was that too many of us are forced to play
roles, or wear masks, different from what our blueprints
would have us to be. We become someone whom we
were not intended to be—the mask, the persona, has
become the person.

Another way to look at individuation is to define it as an
effort to recover as much of the unconscious as possible

and make it usable in a person's life. Jung would be per-turbed at most of us in the Myers-Briggs community for emphasizing so much our four-letter type. I can't imagine he would appreciate at all the license plate on my car that reads *INTJ*. Because for Jung almost as important as our announced letters in our development are our unan-nounced letters—in my case, "E," "S," "F," & "P." Much of what is of value to me as an individual lies unac-cessed in the unconscious. I need to access it and make it usable at the appropriate time. That means having a well-developed dominant function that has for a team-mate an appropriately developed auxiliary function. While these two functions are mainly in the conscious world, they also need working with them a tertiary and an inferior function (See Question 37), both of which have their preponderance in the unconscious world. All four priorities are necessary for a well-developed, indi-viduated person—one who can revel in who he or she is and not have to worry about trying to become that which they are not.

QUESTION 25
How does my age affect my type?

We have a growing data bank on age and type. But, if you are a doctoral candidate in search of a dissertation topic, good studies on the relationship between age and type still need to be done. About all that is clear from the data is that our preferences tend to become clearer as we age (see Question 20).

Harold Grant's model (see "Facing Your Type," p. 13) also sheds some interesting light on age and type. According to Grant, we develop, in a fairly procrustean way our preferences as we mature. In the beginning, we are rela-tively undifferentiated. During grade school years we work on developing what will become our dominant function. Through the years of secondary school and college, our personalities develop their auxiliary functions. Then during young adulthood we pick up interest in our tertiary functions, and around midlife we start working on our inferior functions—that is where the fun really begins. We call that time "midlife crisis" for good and sufficient reasons.

An understanding of type theory and what actually is occurring at these times in our lives can be valuable springboards for inner growth and interpersonal understanding. Many researchers are beginning to explore midlife from the standpoint of our preferences. We could take some valuable tips from the Chinese, for whom the ideograph for "Crisis" signifies both *DANGER* and *OPPORTUNITY*. The same is true of this period in our lives when, for perhaps the first time, we begin to encounter the breadth of those functions rooted more deeply in the unconscious.

I believe too many trainers are far too rigid in their approach to type development. Clearly "things happen" that may accelerate or retard type development. The following are only the general ages at which I find our various functions click in. For me, type is present at birth. I believe it is genetically rooted and that we can chart each of the sixteen types on one of the four levels of the cerebral cortex (See Question 1). For our first conscious years, we try out all of the various inputs and how to respond to them. We may in fact experiment with all of the types in some systematic way, if the systems allow us, as we try to determine what our real preferences are.

About the age of six to ten, we begin to develop our dominant function. We try it out and gain confidence using it. Between the ages of twenty-five to thirty, we develop the auxiliary function. It teams up with the dominant and begins to be part of the pair of preferences in which we

have most confidence. These two provide the ground
floor for our personality. Because they are mostly rooted
in the conscious personality, others who know us see
them as "being us." When I apply for a job during these
young professional years, it is these two letters that I
showcase. Oh, I probably don't put them on a resume, but
I show them in terms of how I interview, the jobs I have
had, the academic work I have completed, how I dress,
and a multitude of interpersonal issues. I demonstrate my
middle two letters. If I get married under the age of thirty,
what my partner sees are my middle two letters—my
dominant and auxiliary. What they see is what they may
get, for a while.

Between the ages of thirty and forty, for the very first
time, a function arises that has been rooted primarily in
the unconscious—we call it the tertiary. It comes along,
knocks on the door, and says: "get ready for an interesting ten years." Because we have never seen it before, the
behaviors associated with it are strange, unaccounted for,
and often out of the ordinary. It is when we are using the
tertiary function that someone might say, "She's not being
herself; what's up?" We know from the data that the
majority of marriages occur before the age of thirty. We
also know that the majority of divorces occur between the
ages of thirty-one and forty. What we hear in our work is,
"Look, he's not the same person I married." Well, in type
theory, he or she is not the same person you married.
They have grown and sometimes grown apart thanks to
the introduction of the tertiary function. The knowledge
of how and why type develops, by the way, is one of several arguments for marrying later in life when the hor-
mones are more muted.

Now, I don't know women very well at all. That has been
my feedback for 55 years; but I do know guys! Here's
what happens in men during this period of "midlife

99

excitement." Their behavior gets a little bizarre. They unbutton a couple more buttons on their shirt and show a little chest hair. Maybe they pop on a gold chain or two, and if their job allows, sport an earring for the first time. To be really cool, they stop wearing socks with their loafers and shift from boxer shorts to jockeys or from white jockeys to purple, green, and red jockey shorts. If they start eating yogurt, take karate lessons, and dare to buy a red sports car, "She knows something is up!" Just go to your local bookstore that hasn't been Amazoned yet and look at all the books that claim to describe how you know if your mate is having an affair; what most of them describe is tertiary behavior. It can be a fairly emotional time, because when we start using the tertiary function it often is expressed in rather emotional, out of control ways.

The tertiary period is when we reevaluate everything. We reevaluate our jobs and careers and often make whole-sale, midlife corrections. We reevaluate relationships and often swap one family for another, one partner for another. Everything becomes "up for grabs." I am not arguing for the rightness of this behavior; I am just offering a rationale for why it happens.

Then the fun really begins when from the age of forty-one to fifty-five, the inferior function comes along and demands for us to deal with it. For many of us, it is like walking on eggs. The appearance of the inferior function in our lives at this stage may well account for the fact that second marriages fail at a much higher rate than first ones.

If all has gone well, and it rarely does, by the time we get to be fifty-five, we will have spent time developing all four functions and know better how to use the appropriate one for the appropriate function.

100

QUESTION 26
Why don't some psychologists accept the MBTI® as a credible tool?

I suppose we all pick the experts we wish to trust, whether the question concerns the nature of God, whether to have open heart surgery or chelation therapy, or whether or not we need to take vitamins to supplement our diets. That may sound a bit "NT" or too cynical a rejoinder, but the questions are not too dissimilar. There are some psychologists who trust reliable, validated instruments to provide useful data and those who believe any such paper and pen "tests" are sheer gimmickry. Jung himself would not take the MBTI®, believing it could not reveal anything of value to a clinician such as himself. As a clinical psychologist, he believed strongly in interview and observation as methodologies. So it is with many clinical psychologists today who are not just a little skeptical about such personality indicators.

Also, we have to realize that for a number of years, Jung was not held in high favor in the psychological community. Freudians and others of non-Jungian persuasion are slow to sing the praises of a practical tool based on an "alien" theory. We also should admit that many of us who are knowledgeable in the field often spend our time working and publishing in the fields of management, teaching, and theology and have not had the impact that we should in serious scholarly journals outside our fields of interest. Thus, it is only recently that articles on the indicator have begun to appear in reputable journals of psychology.

There are also some trite uses made of the MBTI®, and occasionally those using it have not been properly trained to give quality feedback to clients. Suggesting there are ways to "type your pet," for example, or arguing that "fat is typological" doesn't win a lot of kudos from *The Boston*

101

Medical Journal. Any of these problems are sufficient to raise eyebrows among serious scholars. The most popular books in the field, moreover, *Please Understand Me, Type Talk, Life Types*, etc., while often entertaining and insightful, do little to advance the scholarship or research in the field, and the "data" remains anecdotal. These books are written, after all, for the layperson and do not pretend to have the rigor associated with peer-reviewed scholarship.

Regretfully, some trainers talk about the data they have in different areas, when the truth is they have nothing more than an intuitive feel for the data; nor do they have the means of gathering, storing, or assessing the data. We are, in short, often our own worst enemies. If there are some psychologists who are skeptical about the MBTI® and the uses consultants make of it, it is more times than not our own fault.

QUESTION 27
Why do different scales have different maximum scores on forms G?

This is a point that is sometimes missed by those who have taken the MBTI®. A client may assume that a preference strength of 31 for Feeling Judgments is no more clear than a preference strength of 31 for Sensing. That simply is not the case. Because the scale for Sensing goes so much higher than the scale for Feeling Judgments, an "F" of 31 is much clearer than an "S" of 31. The maximums simply depend on the number of questions asked on each scale. In general, the more questions, the more reliable the scale (see Question 4). Knowing the maximum preference strength that can be associated with each of the eight functions and attitudes helps us to see how clear one preference is when compared to the others.

But to say that the maximum limits merely reflect the number of questions asked on any one scale really begs the question. The next question that must be asked then is, "So why have a different number of questions for each scale?" The answer is not a simple one and requires an in-depth knowledge of the mechanics of setting the mid-point on the four dichotomous scales and the process used to establish the weighting of individual responses (some responses those found on the answer keys—have weights of 1 or 2; others carry the weight of 0). The authors spent much of their adult lives ensuring the integrity of this process. The best description of how and why this took place is found in Isabel's own writings and the respective *Manuals*.

Sadly, the publisher has decided to omit the weight of the responses from the manual scoring keys for form M. When the form is computer scored, the weights can be tabulated. Many of us see this as just one more way the publisher is trying to coerce the community to use their computer scoring.

There also has to be a balance between how many questions a person might consent to answer and how many times the authors can find words and situations that reflect psychologically opposed choices with the necessary clarity. The process is not an easy one, and for this reason there is no alternative form of the indicator. At any one time there is only one form F, one form G, or one form M.

QUESTION 28
What percentages of the population report each of the preferences?

Population percentages are tricky for a couple of reasons. Any normative data bank may be skewed, depending on the audiences used to determine the data. Isabel initially reported national norms based on a very limited sample of medical school students and high school students. She suggested early on that the percentages would be:

Extravert 75 %   Introvert 25 %
Sensor 75 %   Intuitive 25 %
Thinking Judger 50 %   Feeling Judger 50 %
Judger 55 %   Perceiver 45 %

It amazes me to see how her early "guestimates" have stood the test of time. By the time the 1985 *Manual* was published the collected samples were into the millions, and the data was refined to a best estimate of:

Extravert 70 %   Introvert 30 %
Sensor 70 %   Intuitive 30 %
Thinking Judger 50 %   Feeling Judger 50 %
Judger 55 %   Perceiver 45 %

By now researchers were also aware of the gender bias that existed in the data on the "T-F" dimension. Roughly two thirds of all those reporting "T" were male and, curiously enough, two thirds of all those reporting "F" were female.

If one were to look at David Keirsey's groupings in *Please Understand Me*, we would find a slight variation in the data. He begins, of course, with temperament groupings and cites the following:
"NF's" 12%, "NT's" 12%, "SJ's" 38%, and "SP's" 38%

He offers no proof for these figures and cites no sample sizes, but the figures make intuitive sense to him. Also, from Keirsey, we can ascertain the rough percentages for each of the sixteen types:

ISTJ, ISFJ, ISTP, ISFP—6% each
INTJ, INFJ, INTP, INFP—1% each
ESTP, ESFP, ESTJ, ESFJ—13% each
ENFP, ENFJ, ENTP, ENTJ—5% each

To this point in the samplings, all the data reported was what researchers call "samples of convenience." In other words there was no effort to create a stratified sample. The numbers of types reported were just an agglomeration of all the groups that various consultants and research groups worked with over the years. The problems with such sampling are myriad. If a consultant routinely worked with military groups, there is a predictable likelihood that their reported data would differ substantially from a firm that typed primarily schoolteachers, clergy, social workers, or medical practitioners. We have known for years that certain types tend to select into certain professions. The self-selection ratio was developed in part to help us understand who was selecting what in terms of group membership.

Beginning with the research leading up to form M, a national sample of persons over the age of eighteen was attempted. Those selected for inclusion were referred to as a national representative sample (NRS). I won't belabor their analysis. If such machinations are important to you, you can find it in the third edition of *The Manual* in part IV, Chapter 7. I find the analysis and attempts at scientific conclusions they draw from it strained at best. Based on the NRS the researchers conclude the following:

	*Male	Female		Male	Female
Extraverts	45.9 %	52.5 %	**Introverts**	54.1%	47.5 %
Sensors	71.7 %	74.9 %	**Intuitives**	28.3 %	25.1 %
Thinkers	56.5 %	24.5 %	**Feelers**	43.5 %	75.5 %
Judgers	52.0 %	56.2 %	**Perceivers**	48.0 %	43.8 %

*(This data is a compilation of that found on pages 157 and 159 of *The Manual*—third edition).

Their combined sample of males and females together is just 3009; furthermore, as the authors admit in *The Manual* and in conference workshops, the sample failed to accomplish either the gender or racial breakouts for which they had hoped. I remain quite skeptical that their extensive efforts to establish a national representative sample accomplished anything more than putting another set of very limited data into the mix.

I'll stick with our company's data bank "of convenience" which is an incredible mix of twenty-seven million people from professions, careers, large and complex organizations, entrepreneurial businesses, Fortune 500 companies, all senior military schools, leadership academies, couples workshops, counseling services, churches, grade school, high school and college students, religious organizations and denominations, gay alliances, civic organizations, all federal agencies in the United States as well as seven other countries, not to mention individuals and families in twenty-nine countries. A partial list of our clients over the last thirteen years is in Appendix A. That sample, in addition to being huge and multicultural, is mostly validated data, unlike what is usually found in *The Manual*, *The Journal of Psychological Type*, or cited at conference workshops. What I will say about that data is that it confirms that Isabel was a prescient genius over 50 years ago, and David Keirsey's sampling—however he arrived at his "guestimates"—is pretty darn accurate.

QUESTION 29
How young can a person be to take the indicator with reliable results?

The 1985 *Manual* describes the reading levels of the questions on Form G and F. There is more at stake, however, than just reading level. Since the questions were initially written for adult populations, the socialization level required to answer some of them is beyond any but mature high school students. Routinely, for anything other than research purposes, the MBTI® ought to be administered to adult populations and older high school students only (my preference is well-functioning 10th graders and higher).

For those younger students, there is also the Murphy-Meisgeier Type Indicator for Children (MMTIC), which has been normed for children with reading levels from the second to the eighth grade (CPP is the source for this indicator as well). The MMTIC uses the same eight dichotomous scales as the MBTI® but has the added feature of a ninth option available on any of the four scales. The additional letter is "U" and stands for undecided, undetermined, undifferentiated, or unknown. Tied votes for any preference on the MBTI® are resolved in favor of "I," "N," "F," or "P" because of the overwhelming cultural pressure to favor "E," "S," "T," or "J." Close scores are not resolved in the traditional manner for children, however, under the conviction that if personality growth means anything, children may opt for the preference of *not preferring.* Until the preference gels, the child prefers "U." The one caution regarding the indicator that is important for users to understand is that "U" does not signify a flaky kid who can't or won't decide. It is *just* as legitimate a choice as are the other eight preferences.

Since what is at stake is not just chronological age but reading level and perhaps socialization level, the MMTIC can sometimes be helpful in organizations that want to use the MBTI® for team building activities but which have a literacy problem among its employees. The questions on the MMTIC are designed to be read to the individual answering the questions if he or she does not yet read. Thus, by using the MMTIC and the MBTI® together, consultants can involve an entire family in the process and not have to isolate those who otherwise could not read the questions on the indicator.

I have experienced one anomaly when using the MMTIC with children. I believe there is a bias in the indicator in favor of "F" over "T." In other words, I have found many children who report "F" as a preference on the MMTIC who, either because of the strong "F" influence in our schools or a bias in the indicator itself, misreport their preferences. Either in interviews when validating their types or subsequently when completing the adult version of the indicator, the same individuals validated a clear preference for "T."

QUESTION 30
Do men and women differ in how they report type?

The one noticeable difference occurs on the "T"-"F" scale (see Question 28). I would suggest that for a more thorough understanding of this difference, particularly in regard to its impact on valuing, that those interested read Carol Gilligan's superb book, *In A Different Voice*. Gilligan writes without an apparent knowledge of type, but her comments about male and female valuing differences and misunderstandings reflects as much the "T"-"F" difference as it does the male-female difference.

Where the difference is in how men and women report their types, is in the choice between the thinking and feeling preferences. The overwhelming social pressure in North America encourages men to be macho, analytical, scientific, and logical; therefore, they are often coerced into reporting "T" on the indicator. Similarly, our culture encourages women to be kind, considerate, nurturing, and empathic; therefore, they are often coerced into reporting "F" on the indicator. For these reasons, whenever a woman reports a slight "F" preference or a man reports a slight "T" preference, I encourage them to look at the opposite choice as well. This is the function pair where I see falsification of type most often (See Question 23).

QUESTION 31
Who besides me gets my results?

Confidentiality is an important issue when discussing the results from the indicator. The APT (Association of Psychological Type) Statement of Ethical Principles underscores several points that users of the indicator must keep in mind. Of cardinal importance is that the decision to take the indicator ought to be voluntary and that the results ought to be returned to the client only. Confidentiality, therefore, is an ethical imperative. Both internal and external consultants will have their mettle tested ensuring that this principle is upheld.

Several organizations, *ESI* included, often return results in sealed envelopes addressed to the clients individually. No one else receives the results. If, for some reason, some of the participants cannot attend the session, I keep their results until a qualified person can explain the results to them. In no event should nametags, desk tents, type tables, or any other listing of types associated with names be prepared in advance and displayed when participants arrive.

Each person has the right to choose whether or not to reveal his or her type, whatever the forum.

Having said all that, I also try to encourage participants to be open about sharing their results. How to do this is always a challenge. Modeling openness is a key to success. Unlike some trainers and consultants, our consultants always announce our types from the start. In my case, it is on my business cards, my stationary, my license plate, and my lapel. If the organization has nametags prepared in advance, I put INTJ on my nametag as well. If there are others who appreciate type in the organization— human resources people, for example—I encourage them to announce their types as well. It is always helpful if a

109

senior business director or vice president can introduce the session and, as part of the introduction, mention his or her type.

As I make my presentation, I am careful to underscore what type is and what it is not, and through a series of personal anecdotes—oftentimes humorous ones—about my friends, family, business associates, and experiences help audiences experience the excitement and non-threatening nature of the results (i.e., there are no bad types, no good types; no smart types, no dumb types; no sick types, no well types; no types suited to the job, no types not suited to the job).

If I or one of my consultants have done this well, by the time participants receive their results they are anxious to share them with those sitting around them. "Yeah, I knew it; I guessed three of the four letters. I'm an ESTJ. What are you?" And the banter begins. It is at this point that I may sometimes ask those who are comfortable doing so to sign in on a large type table I have posted somewhere to the rear of the room. As I send them out for a break, the chart starts to fill. I am careful to stress, however, that there is no obligation whatsoever to share their types.

If, during the presentation, I show a type table of the organization to the group, it will be so they can see how many others of the same or different types there are in the organization. The type table is always devoid of names and gender and merely reflects numbers or percentages of the types or combinations of letters (e.g., "ST," "SF," "NF," "NT"). There are even some times when showing such a generic, scrubbed, type table may be inappropriate—with very small groups for example, where by virtue of sheer numbers one could guess someone's type. No master list of names and types is prepared, and no one receives the results except the individual clients. We, as consultants, are pressured to do so from time to time, and we must decline, citing our ethical obligations and the individual's rights to confidentiality. That has been our contract with the individual, and we must allow no one to void that contract for us.

QUESTION 32
How can knowing my type or the types of others foster better communications?

If you and I see reality differently, we can't have a meaningful conversation. If you and I make our judgments seeing the data through different lenses, we have a hard time understanding one another's positions. If I speak French and you speak Japanese, we have to work very hard, often through non-verbal means to understand one another. If East and West Germans did not have a common language and heritage, reunification would not have occurred as swiftly as it did. Learning about type is, to some degree, analogous to learning to communicate in other languages. Consider this basic cybernetic model of communication:

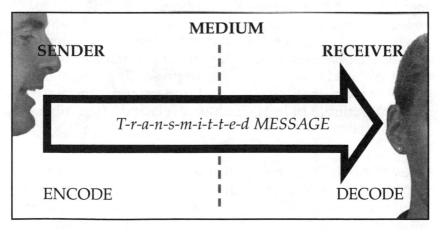

In any communication system, between NASA and the space shuttle or between you and your employees, there

111

is the sender, the message, the receiver, and the medium through which the message is sent. The message may be a thirty-minute marketing presentation, e-mail, an inter-office memo, a counseling session, feedback on an evaluation report, or an award for twenty years of faithful service. In any event, each time a message is sent, it is encoded at the sender's end and decoded at the receiver's end. When I send a message to my office in Hamburg, Germany, or in Monte Verde, Costa Rica, or Shanghai, China, I have to encode it in German or Spanish or Chinese. I have to encode it electronically and bounce it off a satellite or two. When my colleagues in those countries receive the message, they better use the same protocol to decode the message that I used to encode it, or all we get is massive static in the system.

When you and I have a conversation, I as an INTJ encode my view of reality in "N." I encode my judging style in "T." If you happen to be an ESFJ, you decode my message in "S" and "F." Unless we understand the differences, we can't talk. The message is garbled; static scrambles the meaning, and you decode the message using the wrong codebook. Simply stated, the receiver must use the same protocol as the sender. If they don't, there is no communication. That happens every day in your organization and mine. We need to develop skills in presenting material to others in ways that they can best understand, otherwise we communicate only at shallow levels and often misinterpret others.

One approach I use in organizations to underscore this important concept is to teach people how to make presentations to those of other types. Structuring data in specific ways or presenting concepts with clarity involves knowing the preferred style of the person receiving the information. To do less is to risk a lack of understanding or at worst to have a proposal rejected.

On one occasion I was asked to advise an office within the EPA. Their office director and senior staff had recently gone to a congressional committee to make a presentation and, in their terms, had been "blown out of the water." Here's what had happened. The office director and the project leader were both dominant intuitives; one was an INTJ and the other was an ENTP. They were briefing a congressional committee whose chairperson was an ISTJ, and the majority of his staff were also sensors. The committee's comment was classic: *"You haven't begun to answer our questions about the superfund cleanup efforts. We are suspending the hearings. We will expect you to come back next month, and next time bring us data, not science."*

All that had surfaced was an encoding and decoding problem. The scientists had presented a realistic approach to the issue on the table. Their view of reality was couched in intuitive terms. The sensors on the committee wanted a data-based, fact-based, sequentially-developed approach to the solution. It reminds me of the old *Dragnet* television series. Sergeant Jack Webb's persistent mantra was "nothin' but the facts, ma'am, nothin' but the facts."

If I am going to make a presentation to a sensing group, I must emphasize data and information. I will review the facts bearing on the problem and discuss which facts still need to be known. I will try to limit the assumptions required for solving the problem at hand and develop my approach to the problem step by step, in a sequential process. I will lace my presentation with handouts and copies of documents, and I will use overhead or computer-generated presentations to walk the audience through the process in a clear and visual way. If possible, I will use flip charts to reinforce the presented data, so I can leave the necessary data in front of the audience while I speak. I will also ensure that the group has handouts in front of them to refer to during the entire presentation.

113

If I am making a presentation to a mostly intuitive group, my approach has to change. I will take a broader look at the issue. I will limit the data I present, and if using fifty overhead slides with the sensing group, I will use twelve or thirteen slides with the intuitive group. I will present broad concepts and the final answer and let the audience press me for any additional data they may want.

The best analogy I can think of is one of my summer jobs during high school. I worked for one summer in the main post office in Ocean City, New Jersey. My job as a high school junior was to stuff mail into boxes. In the back of the post office at 9th and Wesley Avenue was one large wall covered with hundreds of boxes with various addresses printed under them. My job was to look at the letter and place the letter in the proper box so the letter carriers could go to all the boxes on their routes and organize the delivery quickly and orderly. In retrospect, I would rather wear ski gloves and knit rugs in the dark, but the job paid for my first two cars.

Making a presentation to a sensing group is analogous to building the wall. I will build it box by box down one column and over to the next. After following this methodology for forty rows and seventy columns, I will have a completed wall. If I am making a presentation to intuitives, I will deliver the wall as a *fait accompli* and ask them what else they want to know. I start with the finished product and offer a few essential details.

QUESTION 33
Which types work together best on a team?

Without being prescriptive, about all we can say is that some types are more likely to work together with harmony than others; that's another way of saying there may be a more natural kinship among some types than others. My personal preference, born of experience but substantiated by theory, is that people who have two letters in common, one of which is one of the middle two, make the best partners, teammates, co-trainers, etc. By matching one of the middle two letters, we are sure that the two have at least either their dominant or auxiliary function in common (see Question 41). That kinship, however, *guarantees* nothing.

We know experientially that putting college freshman roommates together using certain compatibility data helps the transition greatly. Several schools also include type data in their decision-making model, and by putting roommates together who have two letters in common greatly reduces attrition freshman year.

We also know that certain temperaments are more compatible than others. Before people have a chance to learn about type and learn to value differences, we can sometimes be unsympathetic about those who have different preferences or combinations of them. "SJ's" and "NT's," for example can initially be like oil and water in the business world. The "SJ's" can be counted on to support the system, support the organization, and support the policies, whereas the "NT's" will delight in challenging the very same things. Sometimes "NT's" can be found meeting at the coffee pot at 2:00 pm laying down odds, making book on how high they can have the "SJ's" jumping by 3:00 pm. "SP's" will see the "NF's" as being flaky and ungrounded and "NF's" can view "SP's" as being harsh and unresponsive to interpersonal concerns.

Again, although such combinations guarantee nothing, I like to see people working together who have two letters in common and two letters different. One of the letters in common, ideally, should be the dominant. This is the model we try to use in our company whenever we have consultants training together. When we engage a company in long term consulting work, we strive to have all the dominants represented when we build our consulting team.

Working with business teams presents some different dilemmas. I do not want teams being selected based on the type of the prospective members. I expect team members to be selected on the basis of experience, expertise, functional background, and the array of background factors that influence who we are. Once the team is in place, however, I want to type them right away so we know which types are present and which types are not so I can understand where the team may get blindsided around certain key issues. Typing is always an after-the-fact approach for me, not prior to the team's coming together.

Having said that, here is where I get myself into trouble with some of the purists in the field. Once all the variables are considered as to why certain people are selected for a team, if I find the team has no feeling judgers ("F's") or no sensors ("S's") on it, I would use type to add some diversity to the team. Fifteen sensors, for example, is not the ideal make-up for a team plotting a long range marketing strategy for a pharmaceutical company. Similarly, twelve intuitives need some sensing help in looking at instructing job specific skills for a manufacturing process. This is considering diversity at its best. Just as ten, middle-aged, pot-bellied white males running a company in central Indiana may not have a lot of insights into how to sell personal care products effectively to Latino or African American females in South Central Los Angeles, so certain types don't always have keen insights into the natural preferences of others.

QUESTION 34
How does stress impact my results?
The answer to this question demands a book. Stress is one

116

of the variables that can skew how you report your preferences. I do not mean minor stress, like, "Oops, I dropped my pencil" kind of stress; I mean major stress. You get fired. You walk into your office in the morning and the *60 Minutes* camera crew is there shooting film of the FBI seizing your computer. Mom has to go into the nursing home for the first time; your handcuffed teenage son pulls up in the back seat of a patrol car; Bambi comes through the windshield of your Lexus; or your twenty-five year-old-daughter moves back in with her two kids—you know, the "bounce back" generation. These kinds of stressors can skew your reported preferences (See Question 6).

Let's get more specific. There is good stress and bad stress. Each of us has an optimum level of stress for high performance. In my previous life in the military, I used to specialize in getting people to that optimum level. When we are "there," sports psychologists call that being "in the Zone." This is the point when we make stress our friend.

Remember the 2002 Winter Olympics in Salt Lake City? When the final competition for the women's figure skating event came around there were three contenders. First there was Michelle Kwan, America's sweetheart and Chevrolet's advertising icon, who was in first place going into the final skate. During the entire week leading up to this night Scott Hamilton, Bob Kostas, and even good old Jim McKay (whom the network had propped up for one last Olympics) had prepared us for her coronation. She had deserved the gold medal in Nagano, we were assured, and would redeem herself in Salt Lake City. In second place was Michelle's chief rival for two years, the Russian skater Irina Slutskaya, and in third place was the American skater Sasha Cohen who, as Scott Hamilton constantly reminded us, "had it all": looks, talent, personality, jumps, and choreography. The NBC cameras couldn't get enough

117

shots of her stretching, pirouetting, and zoning out with headphones backstage prior to the event. In fourth place was the sixteen-year-old Long Islander, Sarah Hughes. The commentators assured us that the Salt Lake experience would stand her in good stead in the future, once she matured.

The result is now history. Michelle Kwan came out with her professional face on. She was the most highly decorated U. S. figure skater in her generation and had too much to prove. Her face showed she was past the optimum level of stress. She fell and had to settle for the bronze. Her rival skated ingloriously, almost fell three times, and looked pained the entire time—stress will do that to you. She took the silver, by default. Sasha Cohen had it all, except a medal, and finished fourth. She had "zoned out." Sixteen-year-old Sarah Hughes skated the "long program" of her very short life, hitting every jump, landing seven triples, including two triple-triple combinations, and dazzling the entire sellout crowd of the Salt Lake Ice Center. Even the two judges from the former Soviet Union joined the other judges unanimously ranking her first and awarding her the gold medal. She was "in the Zone."

Unfortunately, as stress increases, performance drops off precipitously. Let's use type terms to describe this process. When all is going well, our type is our strength. My dominant and auxiliary work together as a team to help me live my life. As stress builds up, our dominant takes a true leadership role and the auxiliary assists in a remarkable way; I really become my type—this phenomenon for me roughly equates to being in the zone. I'll walk off the stage at break time in the middle of a formal presentation to a group of CEO's and presidents and my senior associate, Jeff, will walk up, put his arm around me and say, "Wow, Bill, dynamite presentation! You're hitting on all eight cylinders today." Optimum stress prepares us for optimum performance.

When stress is optimum, I really become my type; the dominant is the major player. As stress increases, I tend to move from left to right along the scale, Furthermore, as I move through a series of fallback positions from dominant to auxiliary to tertiary to inferior, my responses come increasingly from the unconscious. That means the responses are less recognizable, less practiced, possibly more emotional and out of control, and unfamiliar to any one around me and to me, myself. That's when my colleagues say, "Bill's just not himself today," and they are right.

As stress increases, we tend to move through the four Jungian levels as the diagram below suggests:

			Conscious Personality
D O M I N A	A U X I	T	
--N----	-L----	-E----	-I-------- Stress
T	I A R Y	R T I A R Y	N F E R I O R — SHADOW
Unconscious Personality			

When things are going well for me, I am an INTJ and you get the best of that type. When I am under serious stress I tend to flip all four of my letters, and you get the worst possible, immature version of an ESFP out of control. Not a pretty sight, particularly from an INTJ.

Notice also that as I move closer to acting out of my inferior function, I get closer to perhaps running into my shadow (See Question 38). That's stress! Jung suggested years ago that *everyone, at least once in their life, has to deal with their shadow, or their shadow will deal with them.* Since the shadow is that repository of all that we choose not to deal with in the conscious part of our lives, the confrontation on its terms can be devastating. When I choose, on my terms, to deal with my shadow, it can be a source of creativity, excitement, and power. I believe real creativity and high performance entails a conscious practice of teaming up with our shadows (with our dark sides if you are a Star Wars fan). When the shadow deals with us on its terms is when we have a Columbine massacre (or to prolong the SW analogy, it is when Luke Skywalker loses his arm in battle to Darth Vader).

QUESTION 35
Can I tell from their MBTI® results which of my employees will be honest or dishonest?

NO! Fortunately the MBTI® does not measure such things as honesty or dishonesty, right or wrong, sick or well. If it did, few clients would fill it out, and I wouldn't use it. Those who use computerized handwriting analysis—usually European based—or blood types in Asia to assess human performance, claim to be able to make ethical and moral judgments about clients based on those indices, but no such conclusions can be drawn from our psychological type. Each type can be value-centered and each type can be valueless. Martin Luther King, Jr. and Billy Graham can both have preferences for "E," "N," "F," and "J" and so can Adolph Hitler and Cool Aid Jim Jones.

Furthermore the very behavior that I may deem to be admirable, another person, regardless of type, may find abhorrent. The sources of our values are multiple: religion, upbringing, experience, schooling, the generation in which we were value processing, culture, and genetics, just to name a few inputs. The very values that drove Osama Bin Laden and his followers to murder thousands of human beings in the name of Islam on September 11, 2001, caused many others of the same faith to condemn him for his savagery and evil. He may be my same type, but I choose not to occupy the same planet he does and would revel in helping to eliminate him and any one who thinks like him.

One interesting way to look at values is through the lens of temperament. For an "NF," temperament can be a little bit gray, in the best sense of the word. Situation ethics is their realm of activity. An "NF" may choose to act differently to person A than they do to person B given the circumstances and what persons A or B may need to feel affirmed. As an "NT," that approach to life strikes me as bizarre. For the "NT," values can also be a little gray but for a different reason. I am willing to break virtually any rule, as long as there is a greater principle at stake beneath the rule. The principle takes precedence, not the person, and certainly not the rule. For the "SJ," values are probably the clearest. Do you want to know right or wrong? It is listed in volume 3, chapter 12, numbers 1-14. Memorize them and follow them and no one will get hurt or reported. The rules are our friends. Stay within the rules. For the "SP," the heck with the rules; the principles are probably overly complex and stupid, and the people always want special consideration. No, for the "SP," what works is right. They are the ultimate pragmatists! Now, these descriptions are obviously gross oversimplifications, but not by much.

Different types do tend to approach values and ethical decision making differently.

QUESTION 36
Don't "P's" really procrastinate more than "J's"?

This is one of those questions where my answer has tended to change over the years. One of my early mentors in type taught me to say that procrastination is not particularly a "P" issue—that all of us procrastinate around our non-preferences. I believed that for some time and even argued it diligently while teaching in his company's Qualifying Workshops despite frequent evidence to the contrary. I no longer share that perspective. In an effort to affirm all preferences as valuable, and indeed they are, he abused the meaning of the word "procrastinate" out of its intended meaning. Indeed "P's" do procrastinate. They admit it; why shouldn't the "J's"?

To procrastinate means to put off until a later time. All of us at least appear to do that in different aspects of our lives. The introverted intuitive judger, for example, is sometimes experienced as a "P" for this very reason. For example, some time ago I was asked to write an article on ethics for a scholarly journal. My deadline to have the article at the publisher was about three weeks away on a Monday. I had been thinking about what I was going to say for some time but had not yet put pen to paper. The conceptual work was going on inside, but no words were hitting the paper. My wife was worried and my publisher was a little irked by my "procrastination." But what she read as procrastination was real work going on out of sight. The deadline for my article was on a Monday. The Saturday before the article was due, my daughter and I were running on the beach in Virginia Beach, Virginia. Suddenly I stopped and began writing in the sand with a stick. My very perceptive INTP daughter, Ainsley, who had seen similar behavior before and who has a real knack for cutting through the nonsense, said, "Oh, so the ideas finally gelled, huh Dad?" Indeed they had. I returned home, wrote the article, and faxed it before supper on Sunday. Deadlines *are*, after all, deadlines to a "J." Not necessarily to a "P," for whom deadlines are sometimes *signals to begin.*

While the "P" in the type formula does not stand for Procrastinate, "P's" do have a special knack for getting on "J's" nerves by putting things off. There is, after all, so much data for a "P" to consider. "P's" run around much like the robot-turned-human, Johnny 5, in the movie, *Short Circuit,* saying, "OOOO, INPUT!" As the "P" for perceiver suggests, "P's" externalize their perceiving function (either sensing or intuition) and allow the rest of us to benefit from their perceptions. That can be quite helpful in organizations where the tendency is often to get something, anything, done, often without "wasting time" considering all that "extraneous" information. As a result, sometimes all we see are the frustrations associated with the differences.

A friend tells this story about his family. Last Christmas, his "J" daughter asked her "P" mother a simple question: "Mom, can we string cranberries for the Christmas tree this year?" He sat out in his study hearing the question and thought, what a nice homey question. The nuclear family is intact and all is well in the world. Then his "P" wife proceeded to answer the question:

"That's a great question, Honey. We haven't strung cranberries for a long time. I remember, years ago we used to string cranberries all the time. In fact sometimes we would string popcorn and other times cranberries; sometimes we would mix the two. Then, again, we also used to bring the tree in much earlier from the forest. But that's because houses were much colder then than they are now. We didn't have central heating systems and sometimes just used a stove or a fireplace in one room. So the tree would last longer and not lose its needles or become a fire hazard. That also meant that fruit on the tree would keep much longer and not go bad because of the excessive heat. In fact homes were sometimes so cool that people kept all kinds of fresh food in the cellar. Sometimes there were pickle barrels and even dried meat hanging from the rafters. If there was just a dirt floor in the basement, sometimes people even dug holes in the floors and buried potatoes or beets in the ground to keep them fresh during the winter..."

For fifteen minutes, the "P" gave the "J" the history of food in America. When she was all finished, the "J" daughter said: "So Mom, can we string cranberries on the tree this year?" The mom said, "I just told you we could!" To the "J," she hadn't even come close. Because the "J" externalizes the judging function and expects closure and certainty in the answer, YES or NO are the appropriate choices. The "P" thought she had "answered the mail." The "J" knew otherwise.

With all the other functions, the word "procrastinate" is inappropriate. We do not "procrastinate" around our non-preferences; they simply rate further down on our list of priorities. The "S" avoids theory and concept; the "N" avoids the detailed approach. The "T" avoids interpersonal involvement; the "F" avoids critical comment and impersonal analysis. Procrastination is a different issue. Ironically, sometimes, precisely because we know some approaches or activities are non-preferences, we choose to do them first, but because we have not had much practice doing them they come across as awkward or childish.

On a trip to Arkansas some months ago, I worked with a

124

company headed by a "P." His immediate staff was comprised of all "J's." We met for supper at 6:00 pm. During supper, they began to discuss how they should arrange the golf foursomes the next day after my presentation. By midnight, the "P" boss had still not agreed to the various suggestions that had been made. One of the "J's" turned to me before we broke for the night and said, "Bill, you really have your work cut out for you tomorrow. What you just saw is a pattern of every staff meeting we have had for the last two months since he took over."

What the "J" didn't realize yet, was the strength the "P" brought to the organization by preventing premature closure, by encouraging a sorting out of the options. All she saw was the procrastination, and that she saw negatively. Therein lies probably the greatest tension in organizations: *"J's" vs. "P's."* I have had "P's" admit, "You know Bill, my colleagues think I am downright irresponsible. I simply can't structure my life to meet their expectations."

When properly exercised the "P" is vital to the organization. When there is too much of it, the same behavior can enervate. It's much like the old Greek concept of the tragic flaw in drama. The great tragic heroes of ancient literature did not fail because of some sin, vice, or weakness. Their fault was their *hamartia*—their "tragic flaw." It was frequently defined as an *excess of virtue.* The "J" attitude is a virtue. The "P" attitude is a virtue. But while both are potential virtues, an excess of either one can be a real detriment to organizational effectiveness.

QUESTION 37
Why do some of us who are extraverts have such a hard time introducing ourselves to others or sharing personal insights? Aren't we supposed to be gregarious and friendly?
We occasionally assign behavioral characteristics to types

based on assumptions about one or two letters, when in fact those assumed behaviors do not really match our preferences. Such superficiality is unfortunate. This question takes us to the heart of type theory. For each type there is, theoretically, a priority according to which we prefer to use our functions. We refer to them as follows:

> **Dominant**—most preferred, most comfortable, most trustworthy
>
> **Auxiliary**—second most preferred, second most comfortable
>
> **Tertiary**—third most preferred, third most comfortable
>
> **Inferior**—least preferred, least comfortable, most uncontrollable

Each of these functions is also expressed in a characteristic attitude, either extraverted or introverted. All those who are knowledgeable in the field of type agree as to the attitudes of the dominant, auxiliary, and inferior functions. For all extraverted types, the dominant function is extraverted and the auxiliary and the inferior functions are introverted. For all introverts, the dominant function is introverted and the auxiliary and the inferior functions are extraverted.

Where the disagreement exists is in regard to the attitude in which the tertiary function is expressed. Those who authored *The Manual* hold to the view that the tertiary function is introverted for extraverts and extraverted for introverts (p. 18). I, along with the more prominent experts in the field, Grant, Clark, Thompson, and others disagree. We hold to the view that the tertiary function is *always* "in the same attitude as the dominant function." *The Manual* always grants us a footnote to that extent, but that is as far as the authors are willing to go to buck tradition. For us the attitudes are expressed as follows:

For all extraverted types:	For all introverted types:
Dominant is extraverted	Dominant is introverted
Auxiliary is introverted	Auxiliary is extraverted
Tertiary is extraverted	Tertiary is introverted
Inferior is introverted	Inferior is extraverted

Experientially, the viewpoint represented in *The Manual* that the tertiary function is in the same attitude as the auxiliary and the inferior functions makes no sense to me or to those whose judgment I trust. Theoretically, the issue of balance in type theory also leads me to my view. If one way to see balance is to see it as teamwork between the extraverted attitude and the introverted attitude for the dominant and the auxiliary (see Question 15), by extension it would seem logical (I am a "T") that the same balance should exist between the attitudes of the tertiary and the inferior functions (i.e., that one should be expressed in the introverted attitude and one should be expressed in the extraverted attitude). There needs to be balance among those functions derived predominantly from the unconscious as well as among those residing predominantly in the conscious part of our personality.

But to be candid, the tertiary function is the one we know the least about; hence, there is some confusion about its attitude. There are even some who ride the fence here and aver that the tertiary function can have either attitude. This is simply one aspect of type theory on which scholars disagree.

Let's take one particular type for which this question has unusual resonance. The ENFP is often described as gregarious and friendly, but there is also a quiet, reflective—even withdrawn—side to this extraverted type as well. For the ENFP, the following priorities apply:

Dominant—intuition (extraverted)
Auxiliary—feeling judgments (introverted)
Tertiary—thinking judgments (extraverted)
Inferior—sensing (introverted)

By either schema of assigning attitudes to the four functions, the feeling function for the ENFP is introverted, whereas the intuitive function is extraverted. Even though David Keirsey has colored all of our views about the ENFP as gregarious, happy-go-lucky, and personable, the feeling judgments—that interpersonal function—is both introverted and auxiliary, and thus we may not see it, and the ENFP may feel ill at ease "going public" with that side of his or her personality, until they know you better.

QUESTION 38
I hear people talk about "working out of their shadow function." What does that mean?

It means they are confused about the difference between the "shadow" and the "inferior function." The inferior is a function rooted predominantly in the unconscious, that, when we use or have to fall back on, can cause some rocky times until it has a chance to join the team later in life. The shadow is not a function—not a preference; the shadow is an archetype (See Question 64). The difference is keen. It is, by definition, our least preferred function but under a lot of stress, we sometimes revert to using it. Unless we are well developed in type and relatively individuated (see Question 24), we can come across as out of control and fairly primitive in our behavior.

Since the shadow is an archetype, it resides in the unconscious as a pool of potentiality. Archetypes are universal paradigms of meaning, action, possibilities, and energy that the human race has in common. As Johnson tells us,

while they are universal, "They combine in infinite variations to create individual human psyches" (*Inner Work*, p.
11). As all archetypes, the shadow has both universal
applicability as well as individual selectivity.

Unfortunately, the very words we associate with "shadow" are dark, sinister, evil, unknown, lurking, etc., so that
we get an eerie feeling about its potential in our lives.
This view of the shadow, however, is limited. It can have
a positive, catalytic effect in our lives as long as we "deal
with it" on our terms—as Jung suggested we must. This
part of the shadow, Jung called the Golden Shadow. It is
helpful and creative. If the shadow comes to play on its
terms, we are not at all at ease. It seeks to undo us and
cause us harm.

In short, one does not "work out of" his or her shadow.
One only works out of functions. The function closest to
the shadow, the one through which the shadow is most
likely to appear, is the inferior. One can work out of his or
her inferior function. Unfortunately, too many people confuse the two concepts. Naomi Quenk has written some of
the most informative pieces on the shadow. Her work is
always worth reading.

QUESTION 39
How often should I re-take the MBTI®?

It depends on why you are taking it. Probably the first
time a person takes the indicator—untainted by what the
choices might imply—is, all things being equal, the best
look at one's preferences. Each time thereafter, as one's
knowledge of what is being asked by each question
increases, there is a greater risk that, consciously or
unconsciously, a person can skew the results. As more
and more training programs for employees, programs for
executives, graduate schools, in-service workshops for
teachers, and others find the MBTI® to be the valuable tool

it is, people will be taking and retaking the indicator.

Each time a person fills out the indicator, the data can be revealing. Did the results change or stay the same? What happened to your results after the divorce, job change, departure of your daughter to college, pink slip, separation from service, promotion, or midlife crisis? Particularly because we tend to develop more fully our priority of preferences as we grow older (see Questions 20, 24, & 25), subsequent retakes can prove enlightening. If you are taking it more than a couple of times a year, however, except as part of training programs, you may be into too much self-analysis. Maybe it's time to get on with life.

QUESTION 40
Can't I come out any type I want?

Certainly, the more a person understands type theory, psychometrics, and what preferences the various questions are attempting to sort out, the easier it is to answer the questions in accordance with the answers expected from different types. Those persons preferring "N" and "T" seem to have a particular knack for doing this, if not a drive to do so. But trying "to game" the answers flies in the face of reasons for taking the indicator.

First and foremost, the MBTI® is a self-assessment instrument. It may be valuable to be able to understand a colleague's behaviors, learning styles, communication styles, and the raft of issues we use the indicator for, but the principal use it has is to foster self understanding. Trying to come out any type we want may be good sport for certain types, but it begs the question of why we take the instrument to begin with.

Just as an aside, while it is possible to skew the results,

picking a type and answering the questions accordingly is more difficult than might be expected. The indicator is remarkably sophisticated. Can you game it? Sure, but when you do, I can tell. Besides, what's to gain?

QUESTION 41
Is any one of my four letters more important or more influential than the others?

Just as a corporation needs a leader and a ship needs a captain, so the personality needs a boss. According to the theory, each of us early in life selects a preference that Jung called the Dominant or the Superior function to be in charge of the personality. Theoretically, it is our most favored, most accessible, most trustworthy, and if all has gone well, our best developed function. But that is not always the case. Isabel Briggs Myers called it the "General" of the personality (*Gifts Differing*, p. 14). The description in *Gifts Differing* is the most accessible explanation available for understanding this function and how to discover which it is in each of the types (see also Question 37).

Which function is dominant is not arrived at by finding the preference with the clearest strength; indeed, there may be a number of reasons why a person may report a clearer preference for the auxiliary than for the dominant.

The dominant is arrived at theoretically depending on the person's reported preferences for the two attitudes. We use the "J-P" line to determine which of our functions is extraverted. "J's" always extravert their judging function, whether "T" or "F." "P's" always extravert their perceiving function, whether "S" or "N." This step gets us half way to identifying the dominant function. The second step is recognizing that all the extraverted types (those with an "E" for the first letter), extravert their dominant function. All introverts (those with an "I" for the first letter), introvert their dominant function.

The following are the dominant functions for each type

For ISTJ, ISFJ, ESTP, and ESFP,
the **dominant** function is **Sensing**

For INFJ, INTJ, ENFP, and ENTP,
the **dominant** function is **Intuition**

For ISTP, INTP, ESTJ, and ENTJ,
the **dominant** function is **Thinking**

For ISFP, INFP, ESFJ, and ENFJ,
the **dominant** function is **Feeling**

Each of these four groupings will look different in behavior as well as share different interests. Furthermore, the differences will depend on whether the dominant function is expressed in the extraverted or the introverted attitude (see Question 37). With that added dimension, we have moved onto Jungian turf with eight groupings.

For Jung, there existed a typology expressed by the following eight distinctions:

S (e) Dominant extraverted Sensing
S (i) Dominant introverted Sensing
N (e) Dominant extraverted iNtuition
N (i) Dominant introverted iNtuition
T (e) Dominant extraverted Thinking
T (i) Dominant introverted Thinking
F (e) Dominant extraverted Feeling
F (i) Dominant introverted Feeling

Determining the auxiliary, tertiary, and inferior functions is equally logical. Once we identify the dominant function, the auxiliary function is the other one of the middle two letters. If the dominant is a perceiving function, the auxiliary will be a judging function; similarly, if the dominant is a judging function, the auxiliary will be a perceiving function.

Sensing ——————————————— iNtuition
                Perceiving Function

Thinking——————————————— Feeling
                Judging Function

Referring to the above diagram, once we have identified the auxiliary function, the tertiary is on the same line at the opposite end. Likewise, once we have identified the dominant function, the inferior is on the same line at the opposite end. That is as complex as it gets.

QUESTION 42
Can I use Type to hire the right employee for a job?

The APT (Association of Psychological Type) Statement of Ethical Principles makes it clear that psychological type ought not to be used to advantage or disadvantage anyone. Clearly, by that wisdom, it should not be used as the sole criterion for hiring or firing anyone. Moreover, not only would it be improper to hire someone based solely upon type, it would also be irresponsible. Let's say there was a job in my organization that by some process I knew was the perfect job for an ESTJ. I would much rather hire a smart INFP (a four letter opposite) than a dull ESTJ, an ethical INTP than an unethical ESFJ, a mature ISTP than a childish or petty ENFJ, and the list

133

could go on.

Since type reveals nothing about such parameters (intelligence, development, pathology, etc.)—it measures only preferences—it is a poor criterion for hiring or firing or promoting or demoting. On the pragmatic side, should you decide to hire someone or not hire someone based on type, you are likely to have a class action suit filed against you. The predictive nature of the MBTI® on specific job performance has not been demonstrated adequately enough.

QUESTION 43
Should I use my type to choose a career?

It all depends on what you mean by "use." If you mean should ISTJ's become accountants, INTJ's become CEO's, INTP's become scientists, ENFJ's become ministers, and ESTJ's become foremen, the answer is a resounding "No!" Can type be helpful in choosing a career? "Definitely yes!"

All of us have a number of talents and capabilities, likes and dislikes, not dependent on type. To use our types to pick our careers is to limit who we are. There are a number of listings of types by career field and several of the books in the bibliography attempt to catalogue these. In particular the books by Sandra Krebs Hirsh, Charles Martin, and Judith Provost can be good resources for career analysis. By far the best is the Tiegers' book, *Do What You Are.*

Where type can be extremely useful in career choices is in seeing where our interests match the career fields we are considering. Thus, taking the indicator as a college student or high school student can often prove quite beneficial. Where those interests match, the client is much more likely to find that career enjoyable. However, that match in no way guarantees success in the particular job. Empirically, we *can* say where different types are likely to wind up. There is clearly much self selection that occurs in terms of careers. But the fact that many of the same type can be found in the same job does not imply that they are either suited to that job or that they are doing quality work.

Should a person decide to choose a career where very few or none of his or her type are represented, that person may very well have an uphill battle fitting in. On the plus side, however, that person probably has the greatest possible contribution to make.

In short, knowledge of type can be quite valuable in looking at careers to see where a person may find a greater comfort level. It should not, however, be used to steer persons toward or away from any career or profession. That is an improper use of type.

QUESTION 44
Does being an "F" mean that I am more emotional than my "T" associates?

No, not necessarily. Jung did not intend for the term feeling judger, "F," to be associated with emotions any more than he intended for the term thinking judger, "T," to be linked with intelligence. Emotions may well help the "F" to decide rationally just as logic may help the "T" to decide rationally, but persons with either preference may be emotional or unemotional. Both "T" and "F" are what Jung called the "rational functions." If I were to link "being emotional" with any set of preferences, I would tie it to the attitudes of introversion and extraversion. Extraverted "T's," for example, can be much more "emotional" than many introverted "F's."

Also what is at stake is in which attitude the "F" function is expressed. For example, the ENFP (see Question 37), while extraverted as a type, has as an auxiliary function, introverted feeling judgments. The ESFJ, on the other hand, while extraverted, extraverts feeling judgments as the dominant function. All things being equal, the ESFJ comes across as much more "emotional" than the ENFP, yet both are "E's" and both are "F's." The INFJ, while introverted, extraverts the auxiliary function—"F". The INFP, introverts the same function, even though for the INFP "F" is dominant. On par, the INFJ is much more "emotional" than the INFP, who can often be one of the cooler types. And, to complicate things further, just about any extraverted "T" can come across as more "emotional" than any introverted "F."

In brief, no, being an "F" does not mean a person is more emotional than a "T" colleague.

QUESTION 45
Sixteen types are a lot to remember. Do you have any tips for remembering what all these letters mean?

You're right. Many of the programs that consultants use to assist organizations are based on systems of threes or fours. Their sole virtue is that they are relatively easy to remember. The MBTI® uses eight distinct variables that are grouped into sixteen possible personality types. Furthermore, these letters are treated in a number of different pairings when attempting to demonstrate behavioral characteristics. While these letters and meanings make this model of human personality more complex as a system and potentially harder to remember, the possibilities inherent are many fold more. It does, however, take longer to understand the system.

Perhaps the easiest way to begin thinking about type is to remember the first letter as indicating where our energy for life comes from. Everything begins with an energy source, why not our personality? So, we start with Extraversion or Introversion. Next we ask, how do we see reality? That is a fairly important question. The type formula places that letter second as Sensing or iNtuition. The third letter in the type formula, asks how we judge or come to closure about our respective views of reality. We do that by making either Thinking or Feeling judgments. The last letter in the four-letter type formula tells us how much order we like in our lives. Do we prefer order and structure? If so we get a "J" for Judging. Or do we prefer more openness and spontaneity? If that is the case we get a "P" for Perception. Just eight letters, "E, I, S, N, T, F, J, & P" arranged in a logical pattern comprise our types.

QUESTION 46
How does the MBTI® compare with the DISC?

The DISC is one of a half dozen or so of the most popular personality surveys to which business people have been exposed in training seminars. It is often used by salespersons and occasionally finds its way into the military reserve. Unlike the MBTI®, which is a theoretical model, the DISC is behaviorally based. Its chief virtue is that there are just four categories for people to learn rather than the sixteen types required to understand the MBTI®. Its chief drawback, also, is that there are just four categories, and people can't be boxed in so cleverly.

It is possible, however, to relate type to DISC results for those who have been exposed to each. While there is no direct correlation, the following relationships seem to apply:

PPS	Key Words	MBTI®
D (Dominance)	Hearty, frank, decisive, organizers, blunt, problem solvers, confident, results-oriented, administrators	ENTJ ESTJ ENTP ESTP
I (Influence)	Outgoing, friendly, fun, helpful, enthusiastic, improvisers, warm-hearted, talkative, popular, sym-pathetic, persuasive, responsive	ENFJ ESFJ ENFP ESFP
S (Steadiness)	Quiet, friendly, responsive, loyal, persevering, retiring, relaxed, friendly but absorbed, serve the common good	ISFJ INFJ INFP ISFP
C (Compliance)	Serious, orderly, logical, thorough, observing, analyzing, skeptical, impersonal, principles, critical, theoretical, independent, why	INTJ ISTJ ISTP INTP

Those of you familiar with type will recognize the direct fit with some of the sixteen types with the key words listed. At the same time, there are some that do not fit at all.

QUESTION 47
I read criticism from time to time that suggests the MBTI® is little more than a quaint parlor game because all it indicates is positive "traits" about a person. What do you say?

First, what needs to be said is that the indicator does not measure traits; indeed, that is one of the main differences between the indicator and other personality surveys, such as the NEO Personality Inventory, and others. The MBTI®, based on Jung's theory, posits a series of dichotomies all of which are equally valuable and which are "neutral" in regard to health, pathology, intelligence, development, or psychological functioning. Trait theory indicators measure a trait along a continuum (e.g., shy—————gregarious). One side of the spectrum in trait theory is viewed as more desirable than the other. Such is not the case with the four dichotomies that generate our types.

Remember, also, that the MBTI® is a *preference* indicator. Preferences are by their very nature not susceptible to categories of right or wrong. The fact that I have a strong preference for red licorice or lobster doesn't make me a good or bad person. It is not that the indicator just picks up on positive traits, but that those leading workshops on type or giving individual feedback sessions to clients may tend to emphasize just the positive characteristics of each type. That should be the starting point, because the hallmark of type is that it helps to affirm the intrinsic worth of each individual, but as a follow-on, clients must come to respect that for every strength there may be a concomitant weakness.

The ISTJ's keen sense of responsibility, for instance, may, taken to extremes, result in authoritarianism, rigidity, or misdirected compulsivity. The ESTJ's straight-shooting, up front approach to issues may, taken to extremes, become confrontational and abrasive. The ENTP's knack for pushing the boundaries and generating new and creative ideas can result in their breeding stress in organizations. The desire to nurture, to help, to care that we associate with the INFP, can result in guilt because they themselves may not live up to their own passionate idealism.

139

The ENTJ's almost instinctive ability to lead can, when improperly exercised, become dogmatic and blustering, and in the case of General MacArthur, gets you fired by President Truman. In every case, our strengths maximized can become our greatest liabilities.

Yes, there are strengths associated with each of the types. Yes, knowledge of type helps us to learn to cherish diversity. But we dare not be myopic. There are also potential quagmires we all have to avoid. The indicator is faithful in reporting preferences. We must be faithful in interpreting the results.

QUESTION 48
Is there an ideal sequence of events when introducing a group of people to type concepts?

Yes, and here I am indebted to a number of nameless people, students, colleagues, and friends, who have heard me experiment with different approaches over the last seventeen years and didn't complain and to a number of other professionals in the field whose presentations I have heard and evaluated over the years. The approach I use is suitable to virtually any audience but particularly to the business community.

I prefer a full day to introduce the MBTI® to an audience and to have an in-house resource available to help with any follow-on work that might be necessary. The latter often is not available, and the time I am allotted is occasionally much less. What I will describe, therefore, is an approach suitable to a half-day introduction to type. That time frame is the norm for most organizations.

I begin with some general observations:
The unique language I will be introducing (e.g., extraversion, introversion, sensing, intuition, etc).

140

What the MBTI® *is not* and what *it is.*

A brief description of the psychometric properties of the indicator. I limit this to a few comments about the reliability and the validity of the indicator.

A brief explanation of the theory—Jung's belief that there are two primary forms of mental functioning and what that understanding suggests about how we perceive and judge.

I begin with an overview of the eight preferences. This section is the heart of the presentation. I routinely discuss the eight preferences for about two hours, grounding the preferences the entire time in anecdotes about myself, my associates, and those with whom I have worked in the past. This approach not only roots the presentation practically, but it also models the openness I hope will result as people begin voluntarily to discuss their types. Self-deprecating humor also helps to defuse any tensions the audience may have regarding type.

At this point I return the participants' results. To reinforce the obligation I feel toward confidentiality, each person gets a personal report form in a sealed envelope or one that I hand out personally. This approach is fairly time consuming—and "SJ's" can always improve my system for doing this—but it is time I believe is well spent. I also remind the group that no one else gets a copy of the results, and they are free to reveal or not to reveal their results as they see fit.

So far individuals have not had their results in front of them. I do this for two reasons. First, I want the participants to be guessing, as the presentation unfolds, what their reported types might be. Not only does this help me to evaluate the quality of my presentation, but also, and most importantly, it helps the participants to come to terms with the possible differences between reported type and true type (see Questions 2, and 23). For some types (those with "S" & "J" as part of the type formula) once they see results in print, it is like the word of the Lord sent down from Mount Sinai, carved in stone.

The second reason is that were I to hand out the results before I begin, the odds are that participants would tend to focus *just* on their preferences and not on the other four. Since, from my perspective, the basic reason for people to take the indicator is to help understand themselves and others, I want people to focus on all eight preferences, not just their own.

Here is an ideal place to have some of the participants volunteer to participate in exercises that will highlight the differences I have been discussing. I use exercises that point out the differences between the dichotomous pairs. Nothing helps more than this process to underscore the validity of the results and to help those whose preferences are not clear to gain some clarity about their choices.

I then show a type table, by number or percentage only, of all the types represented in the audience.

I conclude with an exercise and some comments that reinforce some behavioral considerations around letter combinations, either function pairs or temperament (see Question 22).

Finally, I conclude with some warnings about what is likely to happen as a result of our time together. *What would be ideal is that participants begin to cherish diversity,* not just give lip service to it. What may happen, however, is that we turn loose on the world a group of zealous amateur psychologists who begin to type everyone and everything in sight. They need to have reinforced the fact that such is not the goal of the indicator and that they do not have the skill or a complete enough understanding of the model to make such judgments.

I have used this same approach thousands of times and have found it to work. I would strongly suggest using as many visual aids (overhead transparencies, slides, PowerPoint presentation, and flip charts) as possible. Those with sensing preferences tend to learn best in this way. As a general rule, intuitives can learn from a sensing approach easier than sensors can learn from an intuitive approach. When in doubt about the make-up of the group, therefore, aim for the sensors. Of course the ideal approach, the one I always request from clients, is that you know which types are present before you begin the presentation. That way you can structure the presentation accordingly.

QUESTION 49
What is the downside of completing the indicator?

This is a great question because while it isn't always asked, it always seems to be lurking in the shadows. Here are some concerns that we often overlook in our zeal to have people take the MBTI®. Any time we use instrumentation of any kind in small groups we open ourselves up to certain disadvantages.

There is always the *fear of exposure.* What does this say about me? Who is going to know? Why are we filling out this form and the office down the hall is not? Are we downsizing or rightsizing again or removing another layer of middle management based on our results? This kind of institutional paranoia is always possible and should be tackled head on.

Such instrumentation encourages "labeling." This is always a possible consequence and one to be avoided. Of course we already do this quite well. I encourage audiences to think about the ways they already label people in damaging ways. All retired military think like..., all southerners are..., all women with short hair are..., all men with beards are..., all Italians, all blacks, all accountants, all.... And the list goes on. So, long before people know anything about psychological type, they are involved in the very human and often damaging activity of labeling other people. In many ways type cuts across those labels and helps us to see value where, otherwise, there might just be stereotype.

Such instrumentation can result in information overload. This objection is certainly valid. There is much to understand about psychological type and Jungian theory. Frequently consultants will overwhelm audiences with the sheer bulk of information or complexity of the system. Consultants and trainers must be sensitive to this issue and know what to communicate and what not to say in a half-day, full-day, or two-day session. I have heard some presenters in a two-to-three hour introduction to type discussing the shadow, the unconscious, inferior functions, Jung's mistress, and the *anima* and *animus.* Such discussions are confusing at best and irresponsible at worst. These concepts have no place in even a one-day introduction to type. Some types reach data overload faster than others. We need to be sensitive to this potential problem.

"Testing" can trigger anxiety and even anger from the "school" connotation. For this reason, participants should be alerted, prior to filling out the indicator, to the non-threatening nature of the MBTI®. It is, in fact, an "indicator," not a "test," despite the unfortunate use of this word

144

by the form's publisher. As long as participants think about the indicator as a test, there will be rights and wrongs associated with the answers. We all learned in school what it felt like to fail or at least to do less well than a friend on a test. To preempt the fear of getting results back, we must be clear about what the MBTI® really is and what it is not.

It may be seen as diverting from key issues. Frequently I hear from a client something like, "Are we going to begin team building on the retreat or just do something that makes us feel good?" There is the assumption that the link between instrumentation and "real" staff development may be specious at best. I make it clear that nothing is more central to teambuilding than self-knowledge. Even if we stop at that point during a retreat, it is a real plus for an organization. Of course, we go much further, but we start with the individual and then branch out to the others he or she touches in the organization.

Perhaps I am over dramatic at times in stating it this way, but I remind audiences of Jung's concern with the whole person and say, "If you are going to die of a heart attack before the age of 45, you are worthless to the organization; if you are unethical, you are worthless to the organization; if you don't really know yourself, you are worthless to the organization." That's the practical foundation for the MBTI®.

So, yes, there are possible disadvantages that may arise from the use of any personality indicator in organizations. If, however, we are responsible in the use of the instrument, and if we communicate the correct information to participants both before and after they fill it out, the advantages by far outstrip the possible disadvantages. Here are just a few clear advantages of the use of instrumentation—whatever the form—in small groups:

1. Enables early, easy learning of a theory
2. Promotes personal involvement
3. Develops early understanding of constructs and terminology
4. Supplies personal feedback earlier than otherwise possible
5. Produces personal commitment to information and feedback
6. Facilitates contracting for new behaviors among participants
7. Fosters open reception of feedback through low threat environment
8. Provides for comparisons of individuals with others and norm groups
9. Promotes involvement with data and feedback process
10. May surface latent issues
11. Allows facilitators to focus and control the group behavior appropriately
12. Facilitates assessment of change over a period of time.

This change is particularly facilitated if it is used in Conjunction with ESI's Organizational Assessment or Diversity Assessment.

QUESTION 50
Is there any significance to the order in which the letters appear in the type formula?

The letters could have appeared in any order at all, but their current order reflects in part the historical development of the theory. For Jung, the chief discriminator was extraversion and introversion. It seems only appropriate, therefore, that "E" or "I" should begin the formula.

Similarly, Jung said there were two primary forms of mental functioning—perception and judgment. Thus, the perceiving function, "S" or "N," comes second, and the judging function, "T" or "F," follows in the third spot. Since the "J"-"P" distinction was added by the authors of the indicator, it is only appropriate that it should occupy the fourth spot. So, while there is nothing magic about the ordering of the letters, their sequence is traditional and also reflects much of the theory(See Question 45).

QUESTION 51
What is the Preference Clarity Index (PCI) on my report form? I never saw this language used before when taking the indicator.

On the early versions of the indicator (forms A-K), the clarity of your preference was expressed by a number called the Preference Strength. Each preference got a number assigned to it based on a doubling formula devised by Isabel Briggs Myers in collaboration with the Educational Testing Service. We looked at the raw scores associated with each of the eight preferences. On each dichotomous pair, we selected the preference with the largest raw score number, doubled it, and either added or subtracted one point depending on which end of the dichotomy scored the highest. Because of the formula used, all preference strengths were expressed as odd numbers.

Beginning with form M, in an effort to downplay the numbers associated with the reported preferences, the publisher abandoned the doubling formula for ascertaining the relative clarity of the preference. The term Preference Strength is, therefore, no longer used with form M or form Q. That raw score, which ranges from 1-30 on each scale, is now referred to as the Preference Clarity Index (PCI). Said differently, it is a numerical representation of the degree of confidence a person can have in each stated preference.

Raw Score Points   Preference Clarity

Extravert—Introvert Scale

11-13	Slight
14-16	Moderate
17-19	Clear
20-21	Very Clear

Sensing—iNtuitve Scale

13-15	Slight
16-20	Moderate
21-24	Clear
25-26	Very Clear

Thinking—Feeling

12-14	Slight
15-18	Moderate
19-22	Clear
23-24	Very Clear

Judging—Perceiving

11-13	Slight
14-17	Moderate
18-20	Clear
21-22	Very Clear

These PCI's can be found on the scoring keys and in the 1998 *Manual* (p. 112).

Once the PCI is identified, one simply looks at which end

of the dichotomy has the highest score and uses that letter as the preference and uses the PCI associated with it to enter a chart to determine if that number suggests a slight, moderate, clear, or very clear preference. Those of you who have scored forms in the past know this is an altogether different approach to arriving at the preference clarity category. There is not much differentiation across the raw score point spread, and even numbers are "OK." It is also important to note that Preference Strength numbers on form F & G do not correlate with the PCI's on Form M.

QUESTION 52
What is the Prediction Ratio (PR)? Is it related to the Preference Clarity Index?

The easy answer is no. Of course to some extent everything is related to everything else on the form, but the Prediction Ratio (PR) is more a research issue that was used as a way of selecting items for inclusion on the form. The use of the Prediction Ratio began with MBTI® form C. Essentially, the PR expresses the probability that any given response which is designed to reflect a particular preference, actually does reflect it and not the opposite one. This methodology was used to evaluate potential responses from form C to form K.

This historically accepted method continued to be used in the early selection of new items for inclusion on form M to weed out responses that did not accurately predict to levels current with form G. After the initial screening, researchers then tried to refine items further by using an Item Response Theory (IRT) parameter called Differential Item Functioning (DIF) to determine if factors such as age or gender would influence choices. The use of the PR and DIF is designed to help ensure that the responses included on the form are the most reflective of that dichotomy and that a person's preferences are always the best fit.

149

QUESTION 53
Do organizations and corporations have Types?

Many people, including me, believe so. Where we differ is in how we ascertain what that type is. For many people, the organization type is the sum of all the individual types represented in those companies. This information can give us some interesting information about the organization, but it is a very limited view. If we look just at the group type (i.e., INFP: more "I's" than "E's," more "N's" than "S's," more "F's" than "T's," and more "P's" than "J's") or the modal type (which of the sixteen types is most represented in the organization) of a company, we run the risk of making some naïve assumptions.

If we were to use that model for ascertaining type, the FBI, Hoechst, A.G., Millipore Corporation, PPG, Bayer Corporation, the U. S. Military, USX, Lockheed Martin, International Specialty Products, the German Military, Compaq Corporation, Caterpillar Corporation, Blue Cross Blue Shield, Raychem, Volvo of Brazil, Regions Bank, and Komatsu would all have the same culture. That is simply not true. The issue must be a bit more complex.

William Bridges, in his book, *The Character of Organizations*, offers a sound model for ascertaining the type of an organization using a Jungian approach. His thirty-six question OCI (Organizational Character Index) gives us a reasonable approach for ascertaining the "type" of an organization. He analogizes the organization to a person and assigns one of the sixteen types to each organization.

In my book *Hannibal, Hummers, and Hot Air Balloons: High Performance Strategies for Tough Times*, I discuss the model we use in ESI, Inc. to ascertain the character of an organization. Type is a primary consideration, but there are several other variables we look at as well. Once we can ascertain the character of the culture that guides the organization we can be much more precise about how they go to market, how they sell, how they plan strategically, and a host of other variables.

QUESTION 54
Can Type be used effectively in diversity education?

Whenever we are tasked with doing diversity training or education in organizations, we use psychological type as a mainstay in the program. Usually, by "diversity," organizations think they want training in legal issues regarding gender, race, age, cultural, physical access, and sexual orientation. It is a limited view but a starting point. We always attempt to expand their view to include a host of other issues. As Roosevelt Thomas taught us many years ago, diversity goes far "beyond race and gender."

Too often, though, organizations avoid the obvious. If we propose diversity education to organizations, we first separate affirmative action from diversity and legal issues from ethical issues. There is both training in diversity requirements and education in issues that affect all of us. There is also the need to look at how an understanding of diversity impacts other major issues such as retention, succession planning, workplace dress, human resources policies, leading a diverse work force, holidays offered, and food prepared in the cafeteria.

Most importantly we always propose adding a full day of training that we call "Introduction to Human Diversity." This day comes before we look at gender, race, culture, ethnicity, sexual orientation, age, single parentness, physical ability and access and those several other very important issues that impact the workplace. For us, human diversity goes to the heart of differences and similarities among people. We use, of course, the Myers-Briggs Type

151

Indicator® for this session.

The virtues of starting with this approach are manifold.
First, and most important, type cuts through in equal
numbers, all the traditional diversity issues except gender.
It makes the point that at heart people are alike and
builds community rather than dividing people into categories. Once we get to the Thinking-Feeling difference, we
lay the groundwork for more experiential work in later
sessions regarding gender. Also, the session on type is
high energy, fun, and engaging. We set the tone for the
rest of diversity education that the sessions will not be
"beating up" on anyone but rather affirming human dig-
nity.

Most white males come to diversity training with as
much enthusiasm as going to their third root canal within
the same week: "I wonder what I have done wrong this
time." People leave the session on type enthused, looking
forward to what they can learn in subsequent sessions.
Type allows a constructive conversation to begin. Finally,
starting with type allows us to look at the need to create a
culture at every level of the organization that encourages
each individual to bring the full power and authority of
their own uniqueness to the workplace to begin to create
a truly high performing culture.

QUESTION 55
Can Type be used to help create teams that are spread out geographically?
We call this creating the Virtual Team and by extension
creating the virtual organization. The very nature of business today dictates that business teams are spread out
geographically. In the case of my corporation, our thirty
to forty consultants have never been in one place at one
time. Yet, given the nature of my business, we all have to
have one hundred percent of the same vision, values, and

norms every place we work, because my name is associated with everything my company does. I have to create a virtual corporation.

Certainly, as we work together, we are aware of our types every minute of our work; it is our core technology and for many of us our life, day by day. That knowledge is invaluable as we work together. That technology is a bit harder to sustain in organizations where you are concerned with getting products or services out the door every day.

The knowledge of your business is easier to transmit these days. We can be spread out geographically and, thanks to SAP, e-mail, websites, and virtual technology, we can still communicate and share data and sometimes applications around the world. What we miss is the personal side of teaming, the face-to-face communication and means of communicating face to face or running down the hall, grabbing six people, and holding a spontaneous team meeting. This is the aspect of virtual team building we have been working on for some time.

We now have a full-time virtual team working on ways to add the social side, the discourse side to virtual team creation, and we have the technology to team up spontaneously 24/7/365 around the world. We can not only share information and technology but see one another (several persons at a time), collaborate, make white board or PowerPoint presentations, and collectively solve problems using virtual conference rooms, streaming video, and voice over IT.

Our internal technology partner, Virtual Reality Meetings, has created a checklist of technology required before we can share our processes with you. If you currently have the following technology, we can bring the same virtual discourse capability to your organization:

Operating System: Windows XP, Windows 2000, Windows ME or Windows 98

Hardware (CPU speed): Pentium/AMD 350 MHz or faster

DirectX: version 6.0 or later

Browser: Internet Explorer (preferred) or Netscape

Full duplex sound card

Headset or microphone

USB Web Cam

Internet connection of DSL or greater

Most of you have these things available on your home computer today. These are the current needs to take you to the virtual team world. How we use them is our proprietary technology which we can share with your team. The pieces of technology may change from time to time, but what will not change is our ability to use Type virtually or in person to change how you do business. While the technology allows a collaboration on the data, knowing a collaborator's Type allows us to increase the knowledge of how and why certain data is being communicated. Without a knowledge of Type, I may misinterpret grossly how and why something is being communicated. As we get more and more sophisticated, virtual technology combined with psychological type will allow us to create a personal, virtual team. It is the wave of the future.You can contact Dr. Rosenberg, our virtual reality guru, at VRMeetings.com.

When I walk into my office in the morning and turn on my computer, my entire multi-national organization, or those I choose to let know, are aware of where I am and whether or not I am available for a meeting, or one-on-

one or one-on-ten team meetings. I can do this with equal ease in Zionsville, Indiana; Antigo, Wisconsin; Sao Paulo, Brazil; Ridgecrest, California; Celle, Germany; Villard de Lans, France; Budapest, Hungary; or Captiva, Florida.

This technology takes us to the heart of (Collaborative) C-Commerce. There is an increasing need among organizations to collaborate and partner on major projects. One pressing question for these organizations is how can they share information in a timely way on complex projects and include everyone who needs to have input in a project. There are a number of systems that are beginning to be developed. One of the best we have found is Bravelo, a C-commerce technology created by one of our partners, BitWise Solutions. You can view it and get a preview of the technology by clicking on the bottom of any page of our company's website at (www.execustrat.com).

QUESTION 56
Can you cite any examples of productivity increases or financial savings gained from using type in a business?

Come with me to a chemical plant in South Carolina that manufactures acetate fibers. In the 1980's and 1990's, it was owned by a German-American corporation. It was also a unionized manufacturing site, comprised of 1,200 employees. The local union was the Amalgamated Clothing and Textile Workers (ACT II), a part of the AFL-CIO.

In 1989 I was on site working with the management and union attempting to set up a structure that met the needs of the contract to develop self-managed work teams. Like so many other organizations, cost was an issue. Fortunately, both the site leadership team and the local union president believed teams might offer a remedy.

155

Unfortunately the site also had a very poor safety record. Two persons died on that site just prior to1989, and a third was permanently maimed. The site manager, a value-centered man whom I had known for two years, was doing everything possible to create a safer working environment. In 1989 he purchased a behavior modification safety program called Operation Zero. In one of the training sessions I was leading, a chemical engineer named Terrence asked me what I knew about this new safety program. I had to confess to him that safety was not one of my company's core competencies, and I had never heard of it. I suggested he contact Dupont or some other company noted for its safety programs and get their assessment.

Terrence pressed me on the issue and said that he knew that we worked in the arena of learning styles and teaching styles and that, although he was just a chemical engineer and did not know much about teaching, he was convinced the company had purchased the wrong safety program for their employees. Something wasn't working. He asked me if I would look at the training materials and evaluate them from the standpoint of what kind of fit it might have with their employees. I agreed and was sent a stack of spiral bound notebooks and videotapes that covered the entire safety training process.

I went through all forty hours of training two or three times and found the materials quite impressive. I sent back a one-sentence fax to the plant manager and Terrence saying "It was the finest safety package I had ever seen; however, it reeked of 'NT'". Terrence and his boss were on the telephone within the hour. They put me on the speakerphone and asked me to explain my comments.

All the managers in the plant had been typed over the

previous year, and I had worked with the site leadership team on type three times prior to this. They all knew type and practiced the language among themselves. I explained that judging from the content of the instructional materials, they had been written by a very knowledgeable expert in the field of safety. No doubt this person was a professor (over 81% of whom are "N's") at some prestigious graduate business school (an "N" institution). He knew the history of safety inside and out. He knew the relationship ("N") between having a near miss go unreported and unanalyzed and having it precipitate into a future accident ("N"). The training package is very "N" in nature. The materials demand a scientific approach to safety ("T"). It is highly analytical ("T") and logically constructed ("T"). When you complete after-action reports, the procedure demands closure ("J") and the site inspections are carefully scheduled ("J"). The entire learning style is independent ("I") and private ("I"). It is an INTJ teaching program. "I like it;" I said. "It meets my needs completely."

"And the problem is?" Terrence asked. "The problem is," I replied, "is that the employees in your plant will be as a minimum, 81% "S" and "J" and "S" and "P" in combinations. And these folks do not learn from an INTJ style, and if you try to teach them in an INTJ style, they will be rebellious in extraordinarily creative ways."

We subsequently typed about two thirds of the plant and found out that I was wrong. They were not 81 % "S" and "J" and "S" and "P"; the figure was 89 %. We then rewrote the forty hours of instructional materials into 4.5 hours but in a style that matched how 89 % learned best. Within a year the plant had gone from the worst safety record in the corporation to the best safety record in the corporation and won the Chairman's award for safety for the best record in the corporation for six consecutive years.

Why did it work? Because Katharine Myers was right in 1917. People learn differently, and it has precious little to do with how smart they are. If you are training in anything in your company and have not thought about psychological type in the process of putting together your training materials, you could be wasting millions of dollars a year and missing from 30 % to 60 % of your employees every year, regardless of how good your trainers might be. You can't afford that!

QUESTION 57
How can we use Type with outdoor adventure training?

We specialize in creating outdoor learning activities that reinforce classroom learnings and help participants stretch themselves individually and personally as well as organizationally. The activity may involve helping to crew a twelve-meter America's Cup boat in St. Maarten's Bay, hiking the Appalachian Trail, taking a white water rafting trip down the Colorado River, paddling a dugout canoe on the Amazon River, dropping eggs from the roof of the Marina Mandarin Hotel in Singapore, orienteering through the French Alps in Villard de Lans, building bridges across gullies in the Great Forest outside Brussels, Belgium, rappelling down a sheer face of a rock wall in Georgia or down the tile façade of a hotel in Shanghai.

At a more pedestrian level, we work with the finest outdoor learning folks in the world at several high ropes courses in the United States as well as in Germany, Belgium, Singapore, the Philippines, Italy, and elsewhere. "Type" is a valuable learning prior to our participating in any outdoor activity. In most of these activities the participants face an element of fear. Usually that fear is of their own making. Dr. Richard Kimball taught me years ago to encourage the participants always to take one step further than they thought they could. Part of our coaching them

158

through the event, demands an understanding of type; different types need support and encouragement offered in different ways.

Whether walking through the jungle at night—it's only called a rain forest in kiddie publications or by those wanting to take some of your dollars for environmental issues—when participants are listening to predators feeding on other mammals, staring into a swirling whirlpool at the bottom of a seven foot drop on a level four rapids, rappelling down a twenty foot wooden wall or a hundred foot cliff at Beaver Creek, Colorado, jumping off of a twenty-five foot "pamper" pole at Grand Cypress Resort in Orlando, Florida, climbing a forty-foot wall at Colorado Springs, Colorado, or helping to crew a twelve-meter boat on a team-building adventure in St. Maarten's Bay in the Caribbean, participants often come face to face with their personal shadow. (See Question 38.) Success requires that they learn how to partner with their shadow for personal growth and team success. Learning how to partner with our dark side for personal and organizational success is the primary technology we use in growing teams.

QUESTION 58
Is Type related to Learning Disabilities?

Anyone who has been a participant in one of our seminars knows our passion about helping children learn more effectively. We have been studying the American educational system for seventeen years and have had the good fortune to work in several public and private school systems across the country. What concerns us most is the glib way children are referred to as LD—learning disabled—when they often merely have a need for a different learning approach.

The data regarding teachers and children has become quite

clear over the years. We know that the general population is about 70 % Sensing and 30 % intuitive. Teachers who elect to teach in grades one through six—early elementary education—are approximately 86 % Sensing. What that means is that the majority of children in the early grades have the support and nurturing from about 86 % of their teachers who understand them, see things the same as they, and test them in ways that make sense. The sensing teachers have elected to teach in those grades because they, themselves, prefer facts and information, and to them learning means amassing facts about a number of subjects. That approach makes sense to the sensing child.

Dittoes, handouts, and other forms of repetitive learning make sense to the sensing child. Sensors learn by repetition and doing; by the way, intuitives do not. I'll come back to them. So, for the first several years of school, the sensing child has material presented and tested in just the right way. Beginning in the middle school, things begin to go haywire for the sensor, because teachers who elect to teach in the so-called middle schools will be, as a minimum, 60 % intuitive. Intuitive teachers have elected to teach in the middle schools because the course work matches their preferences:

Early grades	Middle school
What is 1+1, 2+2?	We get word problems. One train leaves Albany traveling 55 mph; a second train leaves Philly at ….
What is the subject of the sentence?	Write a creative essay.
Break it down	Build it up
True or false tests	True, false, or sometimes questions.

160

It is at this time that the sensing child often brings a note home from the teacher and the note say something like, "I don't know what has happened to Mandy's grades this year; they have taken a real nose dive. Is Mandy having personal problems at home too?" No, Mandy is having teaching problems in the classroom. At one grade, the sensing child loses the support of 86 % of the teachers who phrased things just right, and about two thirds start speaking a different language. That's not fun.

And, the further the sensing child goes, the weirder it gets because the "N"-er it gets. In the middle grades, 60 % of all teachers are "N's." In high school, 70 % of all teachers are "N's"(except for wood shop). By the time you get to college, 75 % of all professors are "N's," regardless of the course work. In graduate school, over 82 % of all professors are "N's." This is not fun for the Sensing student. So, it is not at all unusual that the sensing child moves through the system, gets fed up with the system and after high school says "that's it; I'm out of here." They leave high school and get a job working for General Motors, Crompton Corporation, PPG, BART, Delphi Motor parts, or the U. S. Marines where they can do, make, or produce something. Sensors are the hands-on doers and makers of our society, which is why in any manufacturing site you accumulate type data, you will find at least 85 % of all hourly workers are Sensors. Or the sensor stays in school and pursues a trade or goes to college and gets a degree in finance, accounting, business, or engineering, where they can "S" around at a higher level. At any time in the upper grades, the "S" child is ripe for the label of LD or learning disabled.

That is not to suggest that the intuitive child has it any easier. All the data, as far back as Jean Piaget, suggests that to the extent a child has to use his or her non-preferences exclusively in the growing up years, the develop-

161

ment of the true preference shuts down 100 %. Because the intuitive child is trapped in a predominantly sensing public school system for the first six years, early on, he or she is most likely to be seen by the school as learning disabled at worst or recalcitrant and slow at best.

Give the intuitive child a page of twenty simple addition problems to solve, and if he gets down to number eleven (heck, if he gets down to number seven!) and at that point he understands the concept of addition, to sit there and waste his time answering the rest of those "stupid questions" is the teacher's need, not his. He's got bigger things to do, more important things to do, harder problems to solve. So he doodles, he draws, he fidgets, and he gets up and walks around. The teacher gets upset, the child is not following the rules, and the parent gets the note.

The intuitive child, particularly the "NP" child, is the one most likely to be misdiagnosed as having ADD (attention deficit disorder), and the "SP" child is the one most likely to be misdiagnosed as ADHD—the same affliction with the hyperactivity addition. Today, ADD, ADHD, and all of its clones is an epidemic of labeling our children because they learn best in ways the system is not capable of providing.

When we are called into schools to work with children with learning disabilities, we find at least one in four who has been misdiagnosed and labeled for life. Today about 14 % of elementary school children are labeled as ADD. I have seen some systems where the figure is as high as 30 % and some classes where over half routinely take Ritalin, Dexedrine, Cylert, or a cocktail of the three at lunch each day. Even the American Psychiatric Association suggests that at most 3-4 % of children actually have this learning issue. Some physicians go so far as to say that ADD is a total fabrication. We are ruining our children's lives!

Teachers, parents, physicians, school psychologists, and administrators need to wake up to this incredible mismanagement of young lives.

You might want to investigate this topic further by looking at the books by Hoffman, Armstrong, and O'Dell in the bibliography.

QUESTION 59
How are the skill sets related to leading or managing related to psychological type?

Leadership and Managership are two words that have endured any number of experts pontificating about them over the years. First we praise one and demean the other; the next year the emphasis switches. John Kotter, in his book *A Force For Change: How Leadership Differs From Management*, brings some sanity to the discussion and talks about the need for each in any organization. He lists the basic skill sets for managers and a similar skill set for leaders. Both are valuable for any organization, but each of us has a natural predilection for one over the other—it comes with our types.

According to Kotter, managers plan and budget, organize and staff, control and problem solve, and spend the bulk of their time creating systems of order and predictability. On the other hand, leaders are more concerned with setting direction and envisioning the future. They align, motivate, inspire, and energize others. Their desire to promote change tends to destabilize the organization (pp. 4-6).

Knowing your type, you can see which set of behaviors comes more naturally to you. All types can be both good managers and good leaders, but the behavioral set we associate with managers is much more "S," "T," and "J."

163

The behaviors we associate with leading tend to be more "N," "F," and "P." High performance organizations need a healthy mixture of each. A good executive coach will always help business leaders see the need for personal development and good type development (see Question 24).

QUESTION 60
How can we use Type most effectively when doing managerial coaching?

My personal belief is that, all things being equal, a consultant skilled in type makes the most effective coach for managers and executives. Type is a valuable tool for understanding self and the organization. Success often entails an individual's learning how to leverage his or her intellectual and personal capital to fit the needs of the organization (See Question 53).

In the past, coaching was a remedial activity. The manager, who was assigned a coach, was perceived as experiencing some problem meeting expectations or was seen not fitting in to the job or the organizational culture. The solution was "find her a coach to fix the problem." Even though that is an old style approach to coaching, it still goes on. The skilled coach can use the indicator to type the individual, type the job they are in, and perhaps type the organizational culture to see where the mismatch might be.

If the organization is more enlightened and sees coaching as a positive growth vehicle for high performers, understanding psychological type can be a tremendous learning activity for the individual. The first and foremost use of type that we preach is self-assessment as a way of moving towards self mastery. Too many times in western cultures, managers are too focused on the job, too worried about meeting the bottom line, too pressured to make the numbers that they fail to take time to do serious personal reflection about their strengths and potential liabilities.

And so the typical, hard-charging executive winds up as a vice president at 38. He is on his second or third marriage, the teenage daughter won't talk to him, and his son is in trouble in school every day. What happens along the way is we forget to come to terms with who we are and what we are intended to be. Type can be a great asset in understanding our individual intellectual capital. Perhaps nothing is more important in our ongoing efforts to strive to attain high performance.

QUESTION 61
Have the questions on the indicator always been the same, and, if I take the indicator repeated times, are there alternate versions of the form?

The development of the indicator has progressed systematically since 1942 from form A through form F, and offering several versions of Form C along the way. Form C-3 added item weightings for the first time and form D added word pairs, which, although they lacked in "face validity" actually increased the statistical validity of the form greatly. All the forms from A-E were essentially phased out by the early 1970's. It is unlikely you will ever confront one of these early versions of the indicator. They may be interesting from a historical perspective but have little relation to the question posed.

Beginning with form F, we began to get some standardization in the type community, and throughout the 1970's form F became the standard or "authorized" version. It contained 166 items, including several "research items" scattered throughout the form that were used by researchers as an ongoing bank of questions for validation on future versions as well as for speculation about issues involving health, psychotherapy, and other issues related to personality. For the first time, we had a form with solid validity, high take-retake reliability, and other very respectable psychometric considerations. This form is still available, and you may see it from time to time if you work for a big corporation that hasn't replenished its stock of training materials for several years. If you do not already have form F in stock, there is no reason to buy it or to complete it.

In the early 1970's, the MBTI® scales were restandardized and form G was published by Consulting Psychologists Press (CPP) as the new "Authorized Version" in 1977. This form contained a total of 126 items (40 fewer than form F). Of the 126 questions, only 94 are scored for type; the other 31 questions, again, are there for "other" reasons—either research on medical and therapeutic issues or grist for ongoing item development. Of the 126 core questions that stayed after the revision of form F, one question was substituted on the Extravert-Introvert scale and eight items were changed or reworded for clarity. In order to account for individuals who, for whatever reason, couldn't dedicate twenty minutes to help to understand themselves better, the publisher also rearranged the question order. On form G, the fifty most valid questions come first, and the thirty-one questions not scored for type come last. So, theoretically, a person could just get through the first fifty questions, and we could get valid results for that person's preferences. This was an editorial change that would come back to haunt us in the future.

Most type practitioners I have talked with over the years were quite happy with form G, once they were weaned from the comfort of the old form F. Some researchers have long maintained that form F gave better results for "high performing" individuals, whatever that means, and, indeed, this myth finds its way into some publications on the indicator. Our firm is the world's largest user of the MBTI® in cross-cultural settings, and we have never seen that distinction in the hundreds of thousands of samples we have from forms F and G over the years. As with form F, form G must be professionally scored, either by hand or by computer, and those using the form must have certain credentials in order to purchase this level B restricted use instrument from the publisher.

In the early 1980's, the publisher decided to start introducing self-scoring versions of the indicator. The rationale offered was that some type practitioners often find themselves in workshops where participants have not had a chance to complete the form prior to attending and send it in for computer scoring. They also allowed that even if the practitioner had hand-scoring templates, it took too long to score large groups of people on-site. Hence, they reasoned, a self-scoring version was necessary, and out came the Abbreviated Version (AV) in 1983. Since the publisher laid the groundwork for completing only a fraction of the original questions by putting the most valid fifty questions up front on form G, the AV had just 50 questions. *What a great way for a crock pot and microwave society to gain abbreviated self knowledge*—you find one lying around your training closet, mark it with a skull and cross bones and bury it under your unused mimeograph or carbon paper. Despite some early claims for the form's validity, its psychometric characteristics did not bear up under research scrutiny and the form died a merciful death.

Unfortunately, the concept of a self-scoring version did not die with it. In the place of the AV, the publisher issued a new self-scorable form G with the same 94 questions found on the 126-question form G used to calculate type. This form, the publisher claimed, provided the same

167

results as the form G that had to be scored by computer or templates. Theoretically, that is true. In practice it became anything but true. In some occasions where I have been forced to use the self-scoring version by a client—the only time I would ever use it—I have seen as high as a 32 % error rate when participants score the form. The order of the questions, "E-I," "S-N," "T-F," "J-P," "E-I," "S-N," . . . is too easy to figure out for several types, and the scoring directions are convoluted for other types.

The occasional error rate in scoring, however, is the least of the problems associated with a self-scoring version. The greatest problem is that such a form encourages the use of the indicator without a feedback session on the results. It is far too easy for an internal trainer or consultant to purchase the form and hand it out to employees to complete, without requiring them to attend an individual or group feedback session to explain the results. This happens far too often. We receive requests for this kind of "very inexpensive" introduction to type almost on a monthly basis. Over the years I have met hundreds of people in seminars who relate stories about "taking the Myers-Briggs on their own and figuring out their own results." Such unprofessional and unethical behavior is rampant, and the existence of a self-scoring version contributes to the delinquency. The publisher should withdraw it from the market. It encourages type knowledge without a chance to validate or invalidate the results by talking to a trained user of the form.

In the late 1980's there began a series of attempts to appear to become more sophisticated in scoring our preferences. The first was the Type Differentiation Indicator, developed by researcher Michael Saunders in 1987. In some quarters, this version is referred to colloquially as the "therapist's version" of the MBTI®. His research

168

TABLE 2
TWENTY STEP II SUBSCALES

Extravert—Introvert:
    Initiating—Receiving
    Expressive—Contained
    Gregarious—Intimate
    Participative—Reflective
    Enthusiastic—Quiet

Sensing—iNtuitive:
    Concrete—Abstract
    Realistic—Imaginative
    Practical—Inferential
    Experiential—Theoretical
    Traditional—Original

Thinking—Feeling:
    Logical—Empathetic
    Reasonable—Compassionate
    Questioning—Accommodating
    Critical—Accepting
    Tough—Tender

Judging—Perceiving
    Systematic—Casual
    Planful—Open-ended
    Early Starting—Pressure Prompted
    Scheduled—Spontaneous
    Methodical—Emergent

became form J, sometimes also called the "long form" of the indicator. This 290-item survey packaged all the questions that Isabel Briggs Myers ever validated with her "item analysis methodology." Form J, as did the earlier Type Differentiation Indicator, provided form G results on type but also broke a person's type into a series of subscales. For form J, currently referred to as a Step III analysis, there are twenty-seven subscales—five subscales for each of the four main preference scales ("E-I," "S-N," "T-F," & "J-P") as well as seven additional scales referred to as "Comfort-Discomfort scales." (See Table 2.)

On each of these subscales, you will receive a Polarity Index (a number from 1-100) which indicates your consistency of subscales within your overall type. Wayne Mitchell's pamphlet on the subscales is the best introduction to understanding Step II scoring.

As this form suggests, obtaining one's preferences now takes on an added complexity. Step II, and Step III approaches to type preferences ask us to believe that on the basis of four to six questions we can sort people into twenty or more subscales. Step I scoring of the indicator reveals a person's type preferences and a numerical strength associated with them. These numerical strengths were originally called *"Preference Strengths."* Now with the introduction of the new form M the numbers are referred to as *"Preference Clarity Indices."* The implication of calling this process Step I is that it is just the first step in self knowledge. Now with help from the publisher and substantially more money from you, you can take Steps II and III. The unasked question is, steps to where?

The first of the forms to include the twenty subscales was published in 1989 by Michael Saunders as the Expanded Analysis Report (the EAR). Each of the four scales became further refined into five others. About this time, out came form K with 131 questions. It could be scored with the same templates as form G to obtain a person's type and preference strength, but when submitted to the publisher (for a charge, of course) it could also generate the twenty subscales that Saunders claimed were significant. It was hailed as the best thing since sliced bread by the publisher but is essentially passé with the introduction of forms M and Q. It will be viewed in the future as only a curious historical artifact in the type museum.

In 1998 the form was once again revised. Two sets of items were considered for inclusion, the 290 items in form J and an additional 290 items written by several hands. A decision was made to base selection on *item response theory (IRT)* rather than the previous *item analysis methodology* upon which Isabel and her mother had relied. The 93 items selected for inclusion on form M were selected after what the publisher claims was an extensive validation process. Ultimately 16,000 households were contacted in an effort to establish a national representative sample for the first time in the history of the forms. Of those, 8,000 responses were actually used. Because of the methodology used to select the items and the high *prediction ratio (PR)* claimed for the items, the need for a gender-based scoring on Form M has also been eliminated. Also, there are no "research" or "unscored questions" on form M. Of course there is a corresponding self-scoring form M! Why let go of a bad idea if it sells? *Form M is now considered by the publisher as the Authorized Version,* although most practitioners still prefer the more settled and, I believe, more reliable form G.

In an effort, I suppose, to drive all users of the indicator to the new form M and to web-based scoring of the form, the publisher has increased the price of form G dramatically. As Consulting Psychologists Press tries to consoli-

171

date their power base in the type community and become the sole source for type materials and interpretations, all the prices have been increased substantially, and there is an effort to try to get everyone in the type community to use the publisher's website to complete the forms. All this is certainly in the economic self interest of the publisher, and they are fully in their right to take these actions. Sadly, though, the prices charged by CPP for instruments and scoring services make such use prohibitive for large groups and smaller mom and pop consulting companies.

As with most business issues, I believe it is a case of "follow the money." Why is the form changing so dramatically? The stated arguments are always in favor of research and standards; the reality is probably money. The publisher can now argue the desirability of taking form M afresh since it supercedes form G as the Authorized Version. All those who have taken form G can do it again and fill someone's coffers. I think the emperor has no clothes. But of course, I am an INTJ and known for my cynicism.

The most recent form to make its way into our lexicon is form Q. This is essentially form M, Step II, the former Expanded Analysis Report, parsed by computer **only** to develop the subscales for the client. There has been a lot of hype about this form in print and at conferences. I remain unimpressed so far. To use this form, you must contact the publisher to have it computer scored. There is currently no hand-scored method for practitioners to use, nor, according to CPP, is one planned for the future.

Here are my main concerns about the many changes occurring as the publisher consolidates their power base. For years, the MBTI® has been a remarkable tool for helping individuals learn more about themselves. It has provided incredible insights to individuals, couples, teams, and organizations in helping people work together more

TABLE 3

FORM	ITEMS	SCORING METHOD (S)
F	166	Form F Templates
G	126	Form G Templates or computer for type
J	290	Form F Templates for type
		Publisher's Computer for subscales
K	131	Form G Templates for type
		Publisher's computer for subscales
M	93	Form M Templates for type
		Publisher's computer for Type & subscales
Q	93	Publisher's computer for type & subscales

effectively as we all seek to understand and value the differences of others around us. The form has given us a fairly scientific approach to understand some intangibles that are difficult to quantify. Eight preferences to pick from, four preferences to value, and a relative clarity to our preferences, has been a valuable approach to understanding people. But even with the past technology, some people find eight possible choices and four overall preferences a lot to deal with. It takes a lot of time for some individuals to understand the technology presented. Furthermore, CPP has offered no way to congeal the data from form G, which is the most extensive data bank available for type, with the new form M. I find that very disappointing.

The new forms also strike me as straining the credibility of the indicator. Without a lot more research, we may simply be trying to quantify the unquantifiable. By assigning more numbers and scales than the 93 questions on Form M may justify and pushing the boundaries of our assumptions about human personality, we run the risk of looking silly in the eyes of legitimate researchers. My great respect for the indicator and my appreciation of all the work that Isabel Briggs Myers and Dr. Mary McCaulley® have done through the years to gain credibility for the Myers-Briggs Type Indicator® cause me to be quite skeptical about the current claims being made for the form. *Just because we can sort data into new ways does not imply that we should. We run the risk of undermining years of insights by stretching the indicator out of its limits.*

In summary, the forms in Table 3 are available in English today from the publisher.

Form Q and the required computer scoring may be justified from time to time for executive or managerial coaching, but I find the times few and far between. In the hands of **a skilled** consultant, Forms G and M are all that are required.

If you have just completed the indicator for the first time, and all this discussion seems esoteric and puerile, I am sympathetic. I meet equally confused consultants every week who, themselves, couldn't tell a form F from a form Q, a preference strength from a prediction ratio, who couldn't begin to explain "item response theory," and furthermore couldn't care less. There is both bad news and good news here. The good news is that you won't have to decide. Some qualified user of the indicator will decide which form to administer, because it is the one they have in stock or the one in which they place stock. The bad news is that your consultant may just be purchasing the latest version to become available with no wise discernment as to why she or he is using it. Again, *if you take the MBTI® from ESI, Inc., you will take Form G, in our opinion the best researched form, into the indefinite future.*

QUESTION 62
Who are some famous people I can reference as examples:

Some of the following persons are best guesses and some have actually completed the indicator. I'll let you be the judge which is which.

ISTJ: George Washington, Shaquille O'Neal (#34, L.A. Lakers), Henry Ford, James Baker, Field Marshall Rommel (The Desert Fox), General Montgomery, Gov. Christy Whitman, over one third of all persons in the military and federal agencies, John Ashcroft, and Mariano Rivera (#42, N.Y. Yankees).

ISFJ: Nancy Reagan, George Bush (41), Radar O'Reilly, Johnny Carson, General Omar Bradley, the modal type for spouses (regardless of gender) of military officers and NCO's and corporate executives, and Laura Bush.

ESTJ: Martha Stewart, Joan Rivers, Harry Truman, Archie Bunker, General Norman Schwartzkopf, Angela Pickles, Barbara Bush, and Lucy Van Pelt.

ESFJ: Tiger Woods, Dwight Eisenhower, Felix Unger, S. Claus, Isiah Thomas, Sean Hanidy, George Bush (43), and the Modal type for public school teachers.

INFJ: Thomas Jefferson, Sigmund Freud, Katherine Briggs, Jimmy Carter, General Robert E. Lee, and Jesus of Nazareth.

INFP: Abraham Lincoln, Joan of Arc, Isabel Briggs Myers, and Mahatma Ghandi.

ENFP: William Jefferson Clinton, Snoopy, General Colin

Powell, Julia Roberts, Oprah Winfrey, Will Rogers, Jesse Jackson, Gerald Ford, and former NYC mayor Ed Koch.

ENFJ: Martin Luther King, Jr., Ronald Reagan, Billy Graham, M. Gorbachev, Vladimir Putin, Jim Jones, Carlos Menem, Jose Maria Fugueres, Adolph Hitler, and Jerry Falwell.

INTJ: Richard Nixon, JFK, Dick Cheney, Condaleeza Rice, Alexander Haig, Roslyn Carter, Al Gore, George Dukakis, Thomas Edison, Henry Kissinger, Jack Welsh, and David Letterman.

INTP: Einstein, Theodore Waitt (Chairman of Gateway), Carl Jung, Immanuel Kant, David Keirsey, and Bill Gates.

ENTP: Oscar Madison, Herb Kelleher (SWA), Gallagher, John F. Dulles, and Robin Williams.

ENTJ: Douglas MacArthur, Frank Lloyd Wright, Eleanor Roosevelt, Ollie North, Lou Gerstner, Donald Rumsfeld, and Rush Limbaugh.

ISTP: Red Adair, Evel Knievel, Burt Reynolds, Sandra Bullock, Sam Donaldson, and General Stonewall Jackson.

ISFP: Charlie Brown, Ernest Hemingway, Mother Teresa, St. Francis of Assissi, Steven Segal, George Carlin, and Michael Jackson.

ESTP: Teddy Roosevelt, George Patton, Lee Iacocca, Brett Farve (#4 Green Bay Packers), Jesse Ventura, and Mit Romney (Chairman of the Salt Lake City Winter Olympics.).

ESFP: Richard Branson, Edith Bunker, Gaugin (artist of Tahiti fame), Steve Irwin (the Crocodile Hunter), and Suzanne Somers.

QUESTION 63
Is the Enneagram related to Type?

There is certainly a lot of effort being expended these days to try to relate one system to the other. Certainly, in Europe, the Enneagram is getting a lot of play recently. At all APT Conferences, there are numerous workshops comparing / relating the two forms. There is no one-to-one correlation of the results for a number of reasons. The MBTI® is a rigorously developed instrument that is based on Carl Jung's system of psychology. It has a logical framework and has been scientifically normed over the years.

The Enneagram is most often used in North America in spirituality circles. Unlike the MBTI®, the Enneagram is not meant to be a system that groups certain persons into type-alike groupings. Its basis is in Catholic theology, Jungian psychology, Babylonian folklore, and Sufi mysticism. With such an eclectic and unscientific foundation, it rarely finds its way into the business world or scholarly arenas.

The word's origins help us to understand its philosophy. The word "ennea" in modern Greek is the number nine, and "gramma" means point. With the Enneagram, we represent nine ways of approaching events, people, and the world on a circle. Each of the nine interstices represents a different way of approaching the world and, as with type, each has an up-side and a down-side. The nine styles are:

    1. The Good Person

2. The Loving Person

3. The Effective Person

4. The Original Person

5. The Wise Person

6. The Loyal Person

7. The Joyful Person

8. The Powerful Person, and

9. The Peaceful Person.

Usually those counselors skilled with the Enneagram talk about people being twos, fives, sixes, etc. Since there are nine Enneagram Styles and Eight Jungian Types, it is sometimes intriguing to try to correlate the two systems. Certainly, some of the words, Joyful, Original, Loving, etc., may seem to relate to one of the dominant functions, but the connections ultimately collapse because of the differing philosophical bases.

QUESTION 64
What is an Archetype, and how does it differ from a type?

Most of us probably learned the word archetype in a high school or college literature or myth course. One of the great myth scholars, Joseph Campbell, popularized the concept several decades ago, but the term actually entered that discipline from the depth psychology of Carl Jung. In his psychology, the unconscious is a repository of many things, but some of the most important constituents of that part of the self are a series of archetypes which, when properly accessed, can be powerful contributors to our understanding of self and others.

These archetypes are primordial, often pre-logical, images, which are part of all human beings' racial and

178

cultural pasts and even may be part of our pre-human experiences. These primordial images have been shaped and modified by all peoples over the years and today may be expressed in religion, poetry, dreams, myths or fantasies. Since they exist in all cultures at all times, they can be powerful binding forces on people. The goddess, the witch, the symbolism of the center, religious sacraments, and numerous others are rooted in the collective unconsciousness of all of us.

Type, on the other hand, is a model of human personality. Our four-letter type is mostly in the conscious world. Our four-letter opposite is rooted mostly in the unconscious world. Where these both are impacted by an archetype is most often with one archetype in particular—the Shadow (See Question 38).

QUESTION 65
Now that we have typed the team or the organization, what is the next step?

When an individual completes the indicator, there are natural follow-on steps. These steps may differ based on the reason the individual completed the survey, but for the most part, our follow-on work consists of looking at behavioral consequences of type (See Question 22), Jungian implications of type (See Questions 37, 23, and 24), aging issues (See Questions 20 and 25), or stress (See Question 34).

With teams and larger organizations, the possibilities are myriad. My book *Hannibal, Hummers, and Hot Air Balloons: High Performance Strategies for Tough Times* looks at business high performance from three perspectives: the thirty-thousand foot level, the ten thousand foot level, and up close and personal. To accomplish a level of organizational mastery, teams and larger organizations need to pose several questions:

Framework for High Performance

What is our *Purpose?* Why do we exist and whom do we serve?

What are our *Core Values?* What sets us apart from others and why should you want to do business with us?

What are the *Norms* or *Operating Principles* by which we will hold one another accountable for following our values?

What is our clearly articulated *Vision?* It is the leader's job to make the future visible.

What is our *Strategy* for arriving at the future state? This strategy must include specific short- and long-term goals.

What are our individual *Roles* and *Responsibilities* for meeting those goals?

What are the *Metrics* we are going to establish at every level of the organization to ensure that we are on tract to attain the vision?

Each of these seven critical steps in laying the foundation for high performance has type implications.

Here is the approach I recommend for building on the introduction to type. My premise is that we expect an introduction to type for a team to be as a minimum one full day. That introductory session I will call *Stage I.*

Stage II: Since the half life of any technology like psychological type is pretty brief, I want to reconvene the group within 60 days for a follow-on session that looks at misconceptions that have crept in over the two months and moves the group forward into the area of behavioral consequences. This session is usually a half to a full day.

Stage III: In the interim, we will have begun to roll out the technology to the direct reports of all those present for

180

the first session. We also seize on "targets of opportunity" that may exist. If sales meetings, quality conferences, safety meetings, or regional leadership sessions are already planned, we try to get a half day to a full day in each of these sessions to continue to roll out type through out the organization. This approach will save the organization money and continue to roll out type throughout the organization

Stage IV: I try to get the organization to pick one or two highly visible teams where we can focus our team building efforts and create success stories within the organization that others will want to emulate.

Stage V: Whenever possible, we try to create an internal cadre of trainers to work with us to have in-house experts when we depart the scene. Nothing emasculates a change effort more than having outside consultants continue to do all the training.

Stage VI: The entire time we will be working with the senior leadership of the organization on the seven-part Framework for High Performance so we have some tangible products to present to the organization as a whole.

Stage VII: If the organization does not already have one, we strongly suggest they institute an annual leadership conference including all the leaders of the company to continue to roll out type and build experientially on behavioral changes necessary. Because we specialize in creating experiential learning labs for teams, we will have those present immersed in numerous activities that bring type and high performance alive. In our mind, the two are inextricably linked.

Our main goal is to keep "type" in play. One or two quick, isolated sessions on type will change very little.

The organization immune system is alive and well in most organizations. As soon as a new technology enters the system, the organizational white corpuscles identify it, surround it, isolate it, and attempt to kill it or expel it. Don't let that happen! Team building, like type knowledge, never ends!

QUESTION 66
Now that I know my type, how can I type my family?

Contact us at www.execustrat.com and we can give you the details. We will do it for you by mail or online, but we need to have a conversation with the person(s) completing the indicator, to ensure they understand their results.

LAST THOUGHTS

Understanding psychological type is a work in progress. None of us have all the answers. Some of us just have more questions than others. As I work with type, I become more and more respectful of the work that Isabel and Kathy did years ago. Theirs is a tremendous legacy for those of us working today to uphold. If nothing else, they reminded us that we all have great gifts and that those gifts differ among us. Those of us who truly believe that sentiment share a great spiritual bond across races, cultures, faiths, and differences of every stripe. I am excited to be part of a community of learners who every day strive to awaken the gifts in all of us. I hope our paths cross many times in the coming years.

If you would like to discuss any of my comments in this book or suggest topics for the next inevitable revision, please feel free to contact me at www.execustrat.com or e-mail me at bill.jeffries@execustrat.com or directly at esipres6@earthlink.net. If the old POTS is your preference, call and leave a message at (800) 977-1688. You might even catch me in the office.

APPENDIX I
Bill's Biographical Data

William C. Jeffries is an international consultant and master teacher who specializes in human and organizational behavior. He has been a soldier, scholar, university professor, editor, business leader, and trusted personal coach for prominent leaders around the world. Currently, as the President and Chief Executive Officer of Executive Strategies International, Inc., he leads a diverse team of consultants with interdisciplinary backgrounds who bring global perspectives to the workplace of the future. His undergraduate studies at the United States Military Academy at West Point were in engineering and management, his graduate work in Germany was in nuclear engineering, and his graduate work at Duke University was in language, literature, and values.

His clientele include an international who's who of public officials, Fortune 500 companies, professional athletes, government agencies, universities, the armed forces, public and private schools, and the media in 27 countries. He has developed and taught programs on Leadership In A Changing World for such organizations as Carnegie Mellon University, Hoechst AG, The Boeing Company, The Federal Executive Institute, Bayer, Eastman Kodak, Caterpillar, Digital, Banco Itau, S.A., Unilever, Capital Market Board, General Motors, Hoogovens Steel, PPG, Merck, ISP Singapore & Brazil, Komatsu International, Pfizer, The Senior Executive Association, Lockheed Martin, Ga. Tech, Regions Bank, Rolls Royce, Plc., Lucent Technologies, United Methodist Services for the Aging,

The Department of Defense, The German Federal Government, members of the Saudi Royal Family, and others.

Bill provides counsel as an Executive Coach and consults with the senior leadership of numerous corporations and organizations including Virgin Airlines, BART, The Environmental Protection Agency, Nuclear Regulatory Commission, Lockheed Martin, North American Chemical Corporation, CIA, Pfizer Pharmaceuticals, U. S. Army, Hewlett Packard, Crompton Corporation, AGFA Corporation, Performance Contracting Group, The Food and Drug Administration, Bayer Corporation, Israel Card, AT&T, PNC Bank, Regions Financial Corporation, IBM, Hoechst, AG, National Bank of Kuwait, New York Transit Authority, SBC, Digital Corporation, Rhone Poulenc, Celanese Corporation, Millipore, Medrad, Raychem, J. R. Simplot, Bristol-Myers Squibb, Spirit Cruise Lines, Giant Eagle, and the U. S. Navy.

In addition to his consulting activities, Bill also advises and teaches in several school systems including The Virginia Association of Independent Schools, South Iron, Missouri Public Schools, West Virginia Expert Teachers Academy, Rockhill, South Carolina Public Schools, and the Zionsville, Indiana Public Schools. Bill also teaches in the Graduate School of Education of Old Dominion University, and the Business Schools at USC, The University of Pittsburgh, Louisiana State University, and The University of Georgia. He is also an adjunct faculty member of the Naval War College in the Department of Strategic Studies, The DuPree School of Management at Georgia Tech, and the Graduate School of Industrial Administration at Carnegie Mellon University, where for 13 years he has been the most highly rated professor in The Program for Executives, the program rated by *The Wall Street Journal* as the World's Finest Program for

Developing Effective Global Executive Leadership.

Bill has written on subjects as diverse as New Business Development, Business High Performance, Organizational Change, Russian Literature, Human Ethnology, War and Morality, Poetry, Professional Ethics, Modern American Fiction, Psychological Type, and the Development of High Performance Teams. His book entitled *True To Type* is widely used in several countries as an organizational leader's guide to personality diversity, and his book *Taming the Scorpion: Preparing Business for the Third Millennium* is used as a leader's guide to developing high performance organizations. His latest book is *Hannibal, Hummers, and Hot Air Balloons: High Performance Strategies for Tough Times.* He is currently writing his first war novel, set in Laos and Cambodia in the 1960's.

In his consulting work, Bill specializes in Organizational Change. He regularly works with corporations to assist them in instituting major organizational changes, developing cultures that support productive work teams, and fostering partnering relationships between customers and suppliers. He frequently is called in to assist in wholesale reengineering efforts of manufacturing sites, corporate-wide diversity initiatives, and the change leadership efforts required to make the implementation of SAP and other enterprise-wide changes more effective.

Bill is affiliated with several scholarly and professional organizations including The American Chamber of Commerce in Belgium, The Association of Psychological Type, America's Promise, The Association for the Management of Organizational Design, The Honor Society of Phi Kappa Phi, The Joint Services Conference on Professional Ethics, the Indianapolis Chamber of Commerce, and the Martin Luther King House.

APPENDIX II
Clients

ABB Power Generation, Ltd.

Advantest America, Inc.

Aeronautical Research Laboratory (Taiwan—Republic of China)

AFLAC

Agfa Corporation

Ajinomoto Co, Inc., Tokyo (Japan)

Allegheny Energy

Allstates Trust Bank, Plc (Nigeria)

Alltel

All Union Foreign Economic Association (Technopromexport—Russia)

Alstom

Amalgamated Clothing & Textile Workers

American President Lines

America Online

American Red Cross

Ameritech

Amsterdam Airport Schiphol (The Netherlands)

Ansys, Inc.

Array Technology Corporation

Arthur Anderson

Asheboro, N. C. Public Schools

Asian Peroxides, Ltd.

AT&T
Austrian Energy (Austria)
Bahrain Institute of Banking and Finance (Bahrain)
Ball State University
The Bank of Butterfield (Bermuda)
Bank Ekspor Impor Indonesia Bankexim (Indonesia)
Bank Indonesia (Indonesia)
Banco Itau S. A. (Brazil)
Banco Real de Investimento S/A (Brazil)
Barama Company, Ltd. (Guyana)
Bay Area Rapid Transit
Bay Networks
Bayer Corporation
Be Free Inc.
Bell Laboratories
Bell Northern Research (Canada)
Bell South
Bethlehem Steel Corporation
BitWise Solutions
Blue Cross Blue Shield
Boeing Company
BP Exploration (UK)
BP Oil International, Ltd. (Malaysia)
Bristol-Myers Squibb
British Airways, Gatwick, (UK)
Brooke Bond Lipton India, Ltd. (India)
Brown and Williamson
Byers Engineering
Cadillac Products
Capital Market Board (Turkey)
Carborundum Universal, Ltd. (India)

Caterpillar Corporation
Cavill Power Products Pty., Ltd., (Australia)
Celanese
Centeon
Central Intelligence Agency
Chase Manhattan Bank
Chem Design Corporation
Chemical Bank
Chevrolet Motor Division
Chevron Petroleum Technology Company
Chevron Real Estate management Company
Christopher Newport College
Cia. Vale Do Rio Doce, Rio De Janeiro (Brazil)
CIBA Vision
Cigna Corporation
Clarion
Colorado Springs Utilities
Cominco American Inc.
Computer Science Corporation
Conoco, Inc.
Coromandel Engineering Co., Ltd. (India)
COSA
Croon Elektrotechniek B. V. (Netherlands)
CTR Systems
Crompton Corporation
Cummins Komatsu Engine Co
Davis-Standard Corporation
Defense Information Systems Agency
Defense Mapping Agency
Defense Nuclear Agency
Deloitte & Touche

Delphi Automotive Systems
Delta
Dentsu, Inc. (Japan)
Digital Equipment Corporation, U.S. & (Germany)
DLG (East Jutland)
D. M. Swagerman Advies B. V. (Netherlands)
Duquesne Power & Light Co
Duracell
Dupont de Nemours
East Africa Industries Limited (Kenya)
Eastern Associated Coal Corporation
Eastman Kodak
Eicher, Ltd. (India)
E. I. D. Parry, Ltd. (India)
Ensalso (Italy)
EPDC, Electric Power Development Co. Ltd.
Ernst & Young
Eveready
Federal Executive Institute
Federal Ministry for the Environment, Nature & Nuclear Safety (Germany)
FEMA
First Funding Corporation
Fisher Scientific International, Inc
Ford Motor Company
Foreign Broadcast Information Service
Freeport McMoran Copper & Gold
Freightliner Corporation
GAF
General Motors Corporation
GM Powertrain, Strasbourg (France)

GM Truck Group
General Railway Signal Corporation
Genstar, Inc.
Georgia Power
Geoserve—CITG
Giant Eagle
Giben America
Godrej Soaps Limited (India)
Goodyear Tire & Rubber Co.
Gough, Gough, & Hamer, Ltd. (New Zealand)
Government Property Agency, Hong Kong Government (Hong Kong)
Great Lakes Chemical Corporation
Hampton Roads Publishing Company
Harris Chemical Group
Haworth International
Hewlett-Packard (Latin American Division)
Heinz
Himachal Futuristic Communications, Ltd. (India)
Hindustan Lever, Ltd. (India)
Hoechst, A.G. (Germany)
Honeywell, Inc.
Hong Kong Government (China)
Hoogovens Steel (The Netherlands)
IBM
IBM (Uruguay)
Ida (Ireland)
IMC
Imperial Chemicals Industries, Plc.(UK)
Institute of Nuclear Power Operators
International Management Institute (Ukraine)

International Services Limited (Nigeria)

International Specialty Products, U. S. (Singapore, Brazil, Belgium)

ISI-Dentsu (Japan)

Israel Credit Cards (Israel)

ITESM (Mexico)

Itochu Corporation, Jakarta (Indonesia), Japan

J. R. Simplot Company

Jemico Group of Companies (Uganda)

Joy Mining Machinery

Kolon Industries—Fiber Production (Korea)

Komatsu Ltd. (Japan)

Legent Corporation

Lisberg—CJ Management (Denmark)

L. K. Comstock & Company, Inc.

Lockheed Martin (all divisions)

Lucent Technologies

Macmahon Holdings Ltd. (South Australia)

Maha Rasta Apex Corporation, Ltd.

Mallinckrodt, Inc.

Marconi

Mastech Corporation

Matsa Lumber Company

Mattell Interactive

Mead

Medrad, Inc.

Merck and Co.

Merrill Lynch

Messier Dowty Aerospace

Milliken & Company

Millipore

Minaj Nigeria Limited (Nigeria)
Mingledorf
Ministry of Welfare, Government of India (India)
Mitsubishi Heavy Industries, Ltd. (Japan)
Mitsubishi Motors
Mobil Oil Co, Ltd. (UK)
Murex Investments
Murugappa Group (India)
National Imagery and Mapping Agency (NIMA)
National Mediation Board
National Reconnaissance Office
National Security Agency
National Westminster Bank, PLC (England)
Naval Sea Systems Command
NCR
New York Transit Authority
Nihon Unisys, Ltd. (Japan)
Norfolk Collegiate School, Norfolk, Virginia
North American Chemical Corporation
Office of the Chaplain, USMA
OHM Remediation
Old Dominion University
Orbisphere Labs
Oriental Brewery Co., Ltd. (Korea)
PACCAR Technical Center
Pacific Bell
Pantone, Inc.
Parry Agro Industries, Ltd.
Performance Contracting Corporation
Performance Solutions
Per-Se Technologies

Petroleum Corporation of Jamaica, (Jamaica, W. I.)
Pfizer Corporation
Photocircuits Corporation
Physitron Corporation
PNC Bank
PPG Industries
Price Waterhouse
PT Sriboga Raturaya (Indonesia)
Quest International (Japan)
Rail Transportation Systems, Inc.
Ramon & Demm
Raychem, Ltd.
Rayonier, Inc.
Regent University
Regions Bank
Rhone Poulenc (France)
Rock Hill, South Carolina Public Schools
Roland Berger and Partners, GmbH. (Germany)
Rolls Royce, Plc (UK)
Roman Catholic Diocese of Virginia
Rompetrol (Rumania)
The Rouse Corporation
Roussell Uclef (France)
RPS, Inc.
Samsung Electronics Co, Ltd.
SASIB Railway GRS
SASOL (PTY) Ltd. (South Africa)
Sastech Pty., Ltd.
Saudi Arabian Oil Co. (Saudi Arabia)
SBC
Scientex, L. C.

Scientific Atlanta
Semeg, Ltd. (Brazil)
Senior Executive Institute
Sharp Laboratories of Europe (England)
Shin Caterpillar Mitsubishi
Shindler Management, Ltd.
Singapore Government
Sona Steering Systems, Ltd.
Southern Company
South Iron, Missouri, School System
South Trust Bank
Southwestern Bell Communications
Space and Naval Warfare Systems
SPIRC
Spirit Cruise Lines
Sprint
State Bank of Mauritius (Mauritius)
Sterling Software
Sumitomo Chemical Co., Ltd. (Japan)
Sumitomo Osaka Cement Co., Ltd. (Japan)
Sun Microsystems, Inc. (Hong Kong)
Sun Trust
Tata Exports, Ltd. (India)
Tata Iron and Steel Company (India)
Teamsters, International
Teijin Ltd. (Japan)
Telecordia Technologies
Texaco (Latin America / West Africa)
Texas Instruments
The Timkin Company
Thermacore International, Inc.

Thiokol Corporation
Ticona
TJ Diamond Chain, Ltd. (India)
Transarc Corporation
TRW, Inc.
Tube Instruments of India, Ltd. (India)
Uarco, Inc.
Unilever-Algida-Iglo (Poland)
Unilever (Netherlands)
Union Switch and Signal
Uniroyal Chemical
United Bank of India
United Methodist Services For the Aging
U. S. Air Force
U. S. Airways
U. S. APCA
U. S. Army
U. S. Department of Agriculture
U. S. Department of Commerce
U. S. Department of Defense
U. S. Department of Health and Human Services
U. S. Department of the Interior, Water Resources Board
U. S. Department of State
U. S. Environmental Protection Agency
U. S. Marine Corps
U. S. Navy Seals
U. S. Navy Explosive Ordinance Disposal
U. S. Postal Service
U. S. Silica
U. S. Steel
U. S. X

United Way
Virginia Association of Independent Schools
Vista Chemical Co.
Wacker Siltronics Corporation
Watkins-Johnson Co.
Wells Fargo Bank
Weltravel (Germany)
Western States Machine Co.
West Virginia Expert Teachers Academy
Xerox Corporation
Zionsville, Indiana, Public School System.

I am also indebted to tens of thousands of graduate and undergraduate students and numerous business professionals at several universities where I have taught who have questioned, debated, argued, challenged, and, in other exciting ways, helped to refine my ideas over the years:

The Armed Forces Staff College
Ball State University
Brussels International School
Carnegie Mellon University, Graduate School of Industrial Administration
Christopher Newport College
Georgetown University Medical Center
Georgia Tech University, Dupree School of Management
Industrial College of the Armed Forces
INSEAD
Louisiana State University
National Defense University, Personal Development Programs

Old Dominion University, Graduate School of Education
Regent University
University of Georgia, Regions Leadership University
The University of Richmond
University of Southern California, Graduate Business
School
University of Pittsburgh, Management in Technology
Organizations
United States Army Command and General Staff College
United States Military Academy, West Point
United States Naval War College.
Virginia Military Institute

SELECTED BIBLIOGRAPHY

Some of the following works are cited in the answers to the questions. All, however, should be in the library of any serious student of type. This is not a comprehensive bibliography by any stretch of the imagination. Research on the MBTI® has burgeoned. This list is the best starting point. Those with shoddy research and poor appreciation of theory do not appear in this listing. There are, unfortunately, many of them. If you want a list of books to begin with as a basic reading list go first to those with an asterisk.

Adams, James L. *Conceptual Blockbusting.* New York: Perseus Book Company, 2000.

Armstrong, Thomas. *Seven Kinds of Smart: Identifying and Developing Your Many Intelligences.* New York: Penguin Books, 1993.

_____. *The Myth of the A. D. D. Child: 50 Ways to Improve Your Child's Behavior and Attention Span Without Drugs or Coercion.* New York: Penguin Books, 1995.

Barr, Lee, and Norma Barr. *The Leadership Equation.* Austin TX: Eakin Press, 1989.

Bartlett, Christopher A. and Sumantra Ghoshal. *Managing Across Borders.* Boston: Harvard Business School Press, 1989.

*Bates, Marilyn, and David Keirsey. *Please Understand Me.* Del Mar, CA: Prometheus Book Company, 1978.

Bennet, E. A. *What Jung Really Said.* New York: Schocken Books, 1983.

Berens, Linda V. *The 16 Sixteen Personality Types: Descriptions For Self-Discovery.* Huntington Beach, CA: Telos Publications, 1999.
_____. *Understanding Yourself and Others: An Introduction to Temperament.* Huntington Beach, CA: Telos Publications, 1995.

Bibliography: The Myers-Briggs Type Indicator. Gainesville, FL: CAPT, continually updated listing, published semi-annually.

Bridges, William. *The Character of Organizations: Using Jungian Type in Organizational Development.* Palo Alto, CA: Consulting Psychologists Press, 1992.

Brownsword, Alan. *It Takes All Types.* Herndon, VA: Baytree Publication Company, 1987.

Campbell, Joseph, ed. *The Portable Jung.* New York: Viking Press, 1971.

Demarest, Larry. *Looking at Type in the Workplace.* Gainesville, FL: CAPT, 1997.

Duniho, Terrence. *Wholeness Lies Within.* Gladwyne, PA: Type and Temperament, Inc. 1991.

Gardner, Howard. *Frames of Mind: The Theory of Multiple Intelligences.* New York: Basic Books, Inc., 1985.

_____. *Leading Minds.* New York: Basic Books, 1995.

Gilligan, Carol. *In A Different Voice.* Cambridge, MA: Harvard University Press, 1982.

Giovannoni, Louise C., Linda V. Berens, and Sue A, Cooper. *Introduction to Temperament.* Huntington Beach, CA: Cooper, Berens, 1986.

Golay, Keith. *Learning Patterns and Temperament Styles.* Newport Beach, CA: Manas-Systems, 1982.

Goleman, Daniel. *Emotional Intelligence: Why it Can Matter More Than Intelligence.* New York: Bantam, 1995.

Grant, Harold. *Facing Your Type.*

Gray, John. *Men are from Mars, Women are from Venus.* New York: HarperCollins, 1992.

Hall, Calvin S. and Vernon Nordby. *A Primer of Jungian Psychology.* New York: Viking Books, 1973.

Hartzler, Margaret. *Management Uses of the Myers-Briggs Type Indicator.* Gaithersburg, MD: Type Resources, Inc., 1985.

Hirsh, Sandra Krebs. *Using the Myers-Briggs Type Indicator In Organizations.* Palo Alto, CA: Consulting Psychologists Press, 1985.

_____, and Jean M. Kummerow. *Introduction to Type In Organizations*. Palo Alto, CA: Consulting Psychologists Press, 1987, rev. 1990.

_____. *Lifetypes*. New York: Warner Books, 1989.

Hoffman, Ronald L. Dr. *The Natural Approach to Attention Deficit Disorder (ADD)*. New Canaan, CO: Keats Publishing, 1997.

Isachsen, Olaf, and Linda V. Berens. *Working Together*. Coronado, CA: NEWORLD MANAGEMENT PRESS, 1988.

Jeffries, William C. *Hannibal, Hummers, and Hot Air Balloons: High Performance Strategies for Tough Times*. Indianapolis, IN: ESI, 2001.

_____. *Profiles of the 16 Personality Types*. Noblesville, IN: Buttermilk Ridge Publishing, 2002.

_____. *Taming The Scorpion: Preparing Business for the Third Millennium*. Chapel Hill, NC: Professional Press, 1999.

Johnson, Robert A. *Innerwork*. San Francisco, CA: Harper & Row, 1989.

Journal of Psychological Type. Thomas G. Carskadon, ed. Glenview, IL: Association for Psychological Type. Published quarterly.

Jung, C. G. *Memories, Dreams, and Reflections*. ed. A. Jaffe, New York: Harcourt & Brace, 1923.

Jung, C. G. *Psychological Types*. Trans. by H. G. Baynes, Rev. by R. F. C. Hull. Princeton: Princeton University Press, 1974.

Kotter, John. *A Force For Change: How Leadership Differs From Management*. New York: The Free Press, 1990.

Kroeger, Otto, and Janet M. Thuesen. *Type Talk*. New York: Delacorte Press, 1988.

*Lawrence, Gordon. *People Types and Tiger Stripes*. 2d ed. Gainesville, FL: CAPT, 1982.

Lowen, Walter. *Dichotomies of the Mind: A Systems Science Model of the Mind and Personality*. New York: John Wiley & Sons, 1982.

McCaulley, Mary H. *Introduction to the MBTI for Researchers*. Gainesville, FL: CAPT, 1977.

McCaulley, Mary H. *Jung's Theory of Psychological Types and the Myers-Briggs Type Indicator*. Gainesville, FL: CAPT, 1981.

Macdaid, Gerald P., Mary H. McCaulley, and Richard I. Kainz. *Myers-Briggs Type Indicator Atlas of Type Tables*. Gainesville, FL: CAPT, 1986.

Martin, Charles. *Looking at Type and Careers*. Gainesville, FL: CAPT, 1995.

Morrison, Terri, Wayne A. Conaway, and George A. Borden. *Kiss, Bow, or Shake Hands: How to Do Business in Sixty Countries*. Holbrook, MA: Adams Media Corporation, 1994.

Murphy, Elizabeth. *The Developing Child.* Palo Alto, CA: Consulting Psychologists Press, 1992.

*Myers, Isabel Briggs. *Gifts Differing.* Palo Alto, CA: Consulting Psychologists Press,1980.

_____. *Introduction To Type.* Sixth ed. Palo Alto, CA: Consulting Psychologists Press, 1998.

_____. *Type and Teamwork.* Gainesville, FL: CAPT, 1974.

_____, and Mary H. McCaulley. *Manual: A Guide to the Development and the Use of the Myers-Briggs Type Indicator.* Palo Alto, CA: Consulting Psychologists Press, 1985.

Nardi, Dario. *Multiple Intelligences & Personality Type: Tools and Strategies for Developing Human Potential.* Huntington Beach, FL: Telos Publications, 2001.

O"Dell, Nancy E. and Patricia A. Cook. *Stopping Hyperactivity: A New Solution.* Garden City, NY: Avery Publishing Group, 1997.

Oswald, Roy and Otto Kroeger. *Personality Type and Religious Leadership.* Washington, D.C.: Alban Institute, 1988.

Page, Earle C. *Looking at Type.* Gainesville, FL: CAPT, 1987.

Provost, Judith A., and Scott Anchors. *Applications of The Myers-Briggs Type Indicator in Higher Education.* Palo Alto, CA: Consulting Psychologist Press. 1987.

Quenk, Naomi L. *Beside Ourselves: Our Hidden Personality in Everyday Life.* Palo Alto, CA: Consulting Psychologists Press, 1993.

Schemel, George J., and James A. Borbely. *Facing Your Type.* Wernersville, PA: Typrofile Press, 1982.

Tannen, Deborah. *You Just Don't Understand: Women and Men in Conversation.* New York: Ballantine Books, 1990.

Thomas, Roosevelt. *Beyond Race and Gender.* New York: AMACON, 1991.

Tieger, Paul D. & Barbara Barron-Tieger. *Do What You Are: Discover the Perfect Career for You Through the Secrets of Personality Type.* Boston: Little, Brown and Company. 1992.

The Type Reporter. Susan Scanlon, ed. Published five times per year by Type Reporter Inc., 11314 Chapel Road, Fairfax Station, VA 22039 (703-764-5370).

von Franz, Marie-Louise, and James Hillman. *Lectures on Jung's Typology.* Irving TX: Spring Publications, 1971.

Yabroff, William. *The Inner Image: A Resource for Type Development.* Palo Alto, CA: Consulting Psychologists Press, 1990.